P9-CDF-157

WORKING WITH THE POOR

OTHER BOOKS BY BRYANT L. MYERS

*Walking with the Poor: Principles and Practices
of Transformational Development*

The New Context of World Mission

The Changing Shape of World Mission

WORKING WITH THE POOR

*New Insights and Learnings
from Development Practitioners*

Bryant L. Myers
editor

ISBN 1–887983–12–0

Published by World Vision, 800 West Chestnut Avenue, Monrovia, California 91016–3198, U.S.A.

Printed in the United States of America. Editor and typesetter: Joan Weber Laflamme. Cover design: Steven J. Singley. Cover photo: Winnie Ogana/World Vision.

Contents

97359

PART FOUR
FRONTIERS

PART FIVE
CONCLUSION

Editor and Contributors

Joy Alvarez has worked for World Vision in the Philippines since 1982. During this time she has held various positions and is currently leadership development associate for World Vision's staff development department, as well as the regional coordinator for Leadership 2001 in the Asia Pacific Region. Prior to her work at World Vision, she was at the Institute for Studies in Asian Church and Culture. Ms. Alvarez holds a B.S. degree in psychology from the University of the Philippines.

Elnora Avarientos holds a B.S. degree in social work from the University of the Philippines. She has worked for World Vision for 18 years in various capacities—in human resources development and management, program development and monitoring, and national office leadership and management. Ms. Avarientos is currently regional facilitator for World Vision's Asia Pacific Regional Office, where she provides support, advice and guidance on broad issues of management and ministry. She and her husband, Eugene, have three sons.

David R. Befus lives in Miami with his wife and two children. He holds the M.B.A. from the University of Michigan and the Ph.D. in International Studies from the University of Miami. He has worked in international management since 1979, with both secular and Christian organizations, focusing primarily on the promotion of economic development. He has also taught at the university level, most recently at Westmont College. He worked for World Vision for six years, where he helped start micro credit programs in Latin America, Africa, Eastern Europe and Asia. He is now president of Latin America Mission.

Dirk Booy is the national director of World Vision Tanzania. He previously held positions with the Christian Reformed World Relief Committee in Sierra Leone and Tanzania. Some of his publications include "Institutional Development in Local Organizations: Capacity Building for Sustainability" and "Institutional Development: A Guide for Development Practitioners." He holds the B.A. degree in social economics from Calvin College and the M.A. degree in international rural development planning from the University of Guelph. He and his wife, Joanne, are the parents of three children.

Jayakumar Christian is associate director of World Vision India-North Zone. He is also a professor at the Asian Institute of Christian Communication and adjunct professor at the School of World Mission, Fuller Seminary. Some of his published articles include "Towards a Response to the Urban Poor," "World Views Should Be Analyzed" and "Redefining Urban Poverty." Dr. Christian holds a master's degree in social work from the Madras School of Social Work, a master's degree in divinity at Fuller School of Theology and a doctorate in intercultural studies from the Fuller School of World Missions.

Beris Gwynne is World Vision Australia's group executive for international and indigenous programs. She joined World Vision in 1994 after a distinguished career with the Australian Department of Foreign Affairs and Trade and the Australian Agency for International Development. She holds a bachelor of arts degree from James Cook University and a graduate diploma in international law from the Australian National University. Ms. Gwynne maintains an active interest in international affairs and is a frequent participant in discussions of relief and development issues within the aid industry.

Ravi I. Jayakaran is the zonal associate director for World Vision of India-West Zone. His current work is in the area of transformational development through rural and urban community development, resulting in the establishment of 21 area development programs. He has trained World Vision staff in many countries, as well as officials from various government agencies. Publications he has authored include *PLA in Small Enterprise Development* and *PLA in Urban Situations*. He holds the Ph.D. in veterinary science. He and his wife, Vimla, are the parents of two sons.

Thomas H. McAlpine is World Vision's director for Bible and holistic ministry, working with national offices to discover and encourage ways for Scripture to empower and shape community development. He holds a B.A. in philosophy from the University of California, an M.A. in Semitic languages and literatures from Fuller Theological Seminary and the Ph.D. in Old Testament from Yale University. His background is in campus ministry (Inter Varsity Christian Fellowship). Since joining World Vision in 1984, he has authored two books: *Facing the Powers* and *By Word, Work, and Wonder*. With his wife, Elvice, and son, Tommy, he is a member of the Episcopal Church.

Bryant L. Myers, Ph.D., is vice-president of ministry at World Vision International. Dr. Myers is the author of *The New Context of World Mission*, *The Changing Shape of World Mission* and *Walking with the Poor*.

Sarone Ole Sena is the capacity building director for World Vision Tanzania. He has worked in the area of transformational development for 20 years as a consultant, teacher and facilitator with government and nongovernmental development agencies inside and outside Africa. He holds the Ph.D. in development studies, an M.P.H. in community health and an M.A. in anthropology. For 13 years he was a university professor in Kenya and Canada. He has authored many articles and papers in the area of capacity building and development.

Daniel Ole Shani has a B.A. in business administration from Taylor University and an M.A. in international development management from the School for International Training. His published works of a development nature include *Participation in Development—Learning from the Maasai People's Project in Kenya.*

Siobhan O'Reilly is the conflict and reconciliation officer in the policy and research department of World Vision UK. Her work involves advocacy and parliamentary lobbying on issues of conflict affecting World Vision's work in Africa and the Middle East, as well as engaging in innovative research and debate on the changing nature of humanitarian work in the post–Cold War era. Ms. O'Reilly has a master's degree in development studies. She has worked with Youth With A Mission in Uganda and Christians Abroad in London.

Corina Villacorta was born in Lima, Peru. For 15 years she has worked with World Vision and other nongovernment organizations (NGOs) in Peru, Canada, Guatemala and Costa Rica. Her papers include "The Changes of NGOs in Latin America" and "The Emergent Roles of NGOs: The Relationship with the Business for Profit Sector." She is currently responsible for coordinating World Vision's Leadership 2001 initiative for the Latin America region. She holds a bachelor's degree in social work from the Universidad Nacional Mayor de San Marcos and a master's degree in urban planning, with a concentration in international development, from the University of California at Los Angeles.

Preface

Setting the Table

Bryant L. Myers

ORIGINS

The idea that led to this book was born in a rainstorm in Los Angeles in 1998. I had just finished a speaking engagement at Fuller Theological Seminary and was driving another speaker, my World Vision friend and colleague Nora Avarientos, back to her hotel. As we drove, Nora asked how the research for my book was going. As part of my research process, she had participated in a three-hour phone interview from Bangkok and knew that I had done similar interviews with four other coworkers.

"I'm a little jealous," Nora sighed. "I wish I could have heard what the others shared with you. I've been at training events with some of them, but we've never had a chance to just sit together and share what we're learning."

Nora was right. As one of World Vision's development thinker/practitioners, Nora travels widely doing seminars and being an internal consultant. She has a lot to share and is happy to do it. But, I wondered, when does she get a chance to learn, except on her own? When and where does she have the opportunity to learn from her peers?

"Nora, let me ask you a question," I replied. "If someone organized a meeting for you and the others who are doing the organization's cutting-edge thinking, a meeting at which you would share with each other and reflect on what you are learning, would you come?"

"Of course! It would be wonderful to be able to listen and to talk together, to be the learner and not always the facilitator," she replied.

"Well, I'm going to write to the others, people like Sarone Ole Sena, Jayakumar Christian and Ravi Jayakaran, and see how they'd answer my question. If enough people are interested, I am sure we can discover a way to do something like this."

And so that is what I did. I sent out seven e-mail messages and, much to my surprise, got seven responses within 24 hours. All contained enthusiastic affirmations and some suggestions.

"Great idea. I'd love to come, but everyone must earn his or her way. Just talking is not enough. Others need a chance to listen in. Everyone who comes should be asked to write a paper and to distribute it well in advance," came the reply from Sarone Ole Sena in Tanzania.

I shared this challenge with the others, and they all agreed to proceed as suggested. As an incentive, I told the group that if the papers were of high enough quality, we would publish them so that others in the relief and development profession could "listen in."

World Vision in Austria kindly agreed to host the meeting. I worked with Sarone Ole Sena, Elnora (Nora) Avarientos, Jayakumar Christian and Ravi Jayakaran to choose topics. Writing guidelines were prepared, and papers were written. In May 1998, 15 of us met in Bad Ischl, Austria. Participants presented their papers, spent time in reflection, and gathered for small-group discussions.

THE CENTRAL CONCERN[1]

The central theme of many of the chapters in this book concerns the struggle to find an authentically holistic practice of transformational development. What is it that makes development genuinely holistic? How do the physical and spiritual concerns of holism come together? What makes transformational development distinctively Christian? These are issues we continue to grapple with.

In the early days we simplistically and incorrectly understood *holism* to mean that Christian witness was something to be added to the development mix to make it complete—just another sector, a wedge in the development pie. Over time we realized that this conceptualization was flawed. It implied that all the other development sectors had nothing to do with spiritual things. We were treating spiritual work as a separate sector of life. How had our flawed concept come about?

As the Enlightenment worked itself out in Western culture, one of its most enduring features has been the assumption that we can consider the physical and spiritual realms as separate and distinct from one another. On the one hand, there is the spiritual or supernatural world where God lives and acts, and where we place other gods. This is the world of religion. On the other hand, there is the "real world": the material world where we hear, see, feel, touch and smell. This is the world of science.

Sadly, this is not just a problem for Western folk. This dichotomy between the spiritual and the physical is rapidly becoming a dominant overlay on the world's cultures. Modernity is deeply embedded in the global economic system, which is being extended wherever Coca Cola is sold. This same culture of dichotomies is taught in every classroom where the curriculum is based on Western educational models. Thus most third-world professionals have imbibed this worldview as an unspoken part of their professional training.

This framework of separated areas of life is also deeply embedded in the Western part of the Christian church. On Sunday morning, or during our devotional or prayer life, we operate in the spiritual realm. The rest of the week, and in our professional lives, we operate in the physical realm and, hence, unwittingly act like functional atheists. Simply being Christian does not heal our dichotomous understanding of our world.

Lesslie Newbigin has shown how this separation of the physical and spiritual realms explains a wide range of the dichotomies that are prevalent in the modern worldview.[2] For example, the spiritual world is the arena of sacred revelation, which we know by believing. The real world where we hear, see, feel and touch is where scientific observation allows us to know things with certainty. Faith and religion are part of the spiritual world, while reason and science provide the explanations in the real world. The spiritual world is an interior, private place; the real world is an exterior, public place. This means that values are a private matter of personal choice, having no relevance in the public square where politics and economics reign. Publicly, we only need to agree on the facts. The church has succumbed to this modern worldview and has allowed itself to be relegated to the spiritual world, while the state and other human institutions assume responsibility for what happens in everyday life.

Spiritual	Material
Revelation and believing	Observation and knowing
Faith	Reason
Religion	Science
Private and personal	Public
Values	Facts
Church	State

Figure 1: The dichotomies of the modern worldview.

Modernity's separation of the physical and spiritual realms is part of the explanation for how we have come to understand Christian witness, and specifically evangelism, as being unrelated to community development. Loving God is spiritual work, and loving neighbors takes place in the material world. So evangelism (restoring people's relationship with God) is spiritual work, while social action (restoring just economic, social and political relationships among people) is not. This false dichotomy leads Christians to believe that God's redemptive work takes place only in the spiritual realm, while the world is left, seemingly, to the devil.

The Christian development agency is not immune to this phenomenon. We express our captivity to a modern worldview when we say that holistic ministry means combining Christian witness (meeting spiritual need) with relief and development (meeting physical need), as if these were divisible realms and activities. Then we make it worse by insisting that the church do the former, while the development agency does the latter. By so doing we declare development independent of religion, something most of us do not really believe.

Paul Hiebert has developed a very helpful framework that compares the worldviews of modern and traditional cultures.[3]

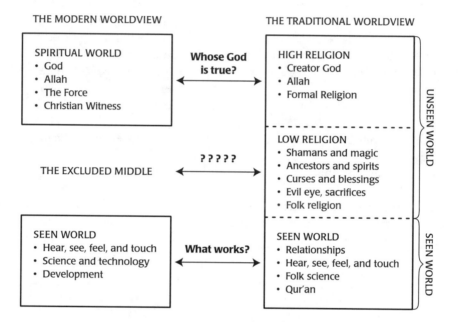

Figure 2: Modern and traditional worldviews.
(Adapted from Hiebert, "The Flaw of the Excluded Middle")

He portrays the modern worldview as two tiered, with the physical and spiritual worlds completely separated. The traditional worldview is holistic, with the spiritual and material worlds interrelated in a seamless whole. The world of high religion is occupied by the great gods, who should not be bothered or disturbed. The interrelationship between the seen and unseen worlds is mediated by shamans, sacred books, spirits and others who have access to both worlds. This is the world of curses, amulets, charms and other attempts to bargain with or "handle" the unseen world.

While the modern world has something to say about high religion and about the physical world, it has nothing to say to the world of folk religion. We suffer from what Hiebert calls "the excluded middle." We no longer believe in ancestors, spirits, the demonic and the unseen. That's all super-stition and ignorance, after all. Yet most traditional cultures spend a lot of time being concerned about this world and locate cause and effect there. This excluded middle from a development perspective is a blind spot. We fail to hear the community's story about the unseen world, and we fail to have answers that, in their minds, adequately take this world into account.

For Christians, it should be humbling to note that the biblical worldview is closer to the worldview of traditional cultures than it is to the modern worldview.[4] The biblical worldview is holistic in the sense that the physical world is never understood as being disconnected or separate from the spiri-tual world and the rule of the God who created it. Moreover, Christ—the creator, sustainer and redeemer of creation—is both in us and interceding for us at the right hand of God the Father. The fact that the Word became flesh explodes the claim that the spiritual and physical can be separated meaningfully.

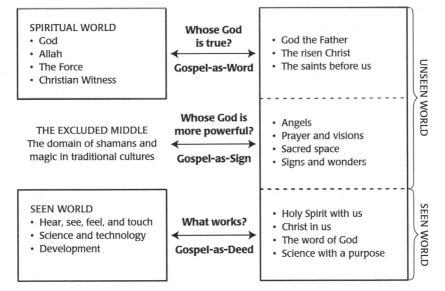

Figure 3: Contrasting modern and biblical worldviews.

This comparison also calls attention to the fact that the critical ques-tions change depending on the level at which one is functioning. The gospel addresses the question of truth with gospel-as-word, the truth of God. The gospel addresses questions of power with the gospel-as-sign, the power of God. At the material level of empiricism, the biblical worldview answers the question, What works?, with good deeds that ex-press the love of God.

This reveals another level of the problem modernity poses to Christian mission. When we separate the spiritual from the physical, not only do we separate evangelism from development, but we separate gospel-as-word from the gospel-as-deed and provide no home for gospel-as-sign. In the spiritual realm the critical question is, Whose God is the true God?, and the answer is an idea. This frame allows us to reduce the gospel message to propositional truth, even a set of "spiritual laws." Christian witness is reduced to words and speaking.

At the level of the physical world, the question is, What works? The answer comes in the form of effective methods and good technology. Deeds and doing are the real thing. We then reduce the gospel message and evangelism to working for justice or saving God's creation.

Separating gospel-as-word, gospel-as-deed and gospel-as-sign has serious consequences. In cultures in which words have lost their meaning, as is often the case in the West, deeds are necessary to verify what the words mean. Saying we are Christian is ambiguous, because almost everyone claims to be Christian. If we want to know what people mean when they say they are Christian, we look at the quality of their lives. The way we live and act declares to others what we mean when we say we are Christians.

In other cultures deeds can be ambiguous. Whether we speak or not, people receive a message. Discovering water in the desert is a miracle, and animist cultures often interpret the technology that brings it as magic and witchcraft.[5] Development technology, without accompanying words to interpret its good deeds, can result in glory being given to clever or "magical" soil scientists and hydrologists rather than to God.

We should also note the inadequate way the modern worldview deals with signs. Because there is no place for the appearance of the supernatural in the physical world, there is no home for signs and miracles. The existential question for most animists has little to do with truth; it has to do with power. Since cause is located in the unseen or spiritual world, the critical question is, Whose god is more powerful? The fact that charismatic and Pentecostal folk have an answer for this question is a major part of the reason why they are the fastest growing expression of the church today. The inability of the modern world to deal with signs and miracles makes it very difficult for carriers of modernity, such as development practitioners, to carry out meaningful conversations with people who hold a traditional or animist worldview. The development practitioner thinks people are sick because of germs and dirty water, while the people believe they are sick because of curses and witchcraft.

Therefore, in dealing with the gospel message we cannot separate word, deed and sign without truncating our message. Words clarify the meaning of deeds. Deeds verify the meaning of words. Most critically, signs announce the presence and power of One who is radically other and who is both the true source of all good deeds and the author of the only words that bring life in its fullest.

The chapters in this book tell the story of development practitioners struggling to overcome this modern problem and to find a way toward a more genuinely holistic approach to helping the poor.

OUTLINING THE PATH

The book begins with a chapter by Jayakumar Christian on understanding poverty. The way we understand poverty determines to a large degree the way we respond to poverty. If our understanding of poverty is not holistic and not biblically sound, it is difficult for our transformational development to be holistic and biblical.

Christian offers a family of ideas about the nature and causes of poverty that breaks us free from the material language and definitions that tend to dominate conversations about poverty. Christian believes that the poor fundamentally experience poverty as a marring of their identity, and this marring is caused by the grind of being poor and also by being captive to the god-complexes of the non-poor. Christian's chapter sets the stage for the others, as they address methodologies for development.

Development methodologies

With this foundation of understanding poverty, the book moves to three chapters on development methodologies: Ravi Jayakaran on holistic Participatory Learning and Action (PLA); Sarone Ole Sena and Dirk Booy on Appreciative Inquiry (AI); and Joy Alvarez, Elnora Avarientos and Thomas McAlpine on using the Bible in transformational development.

Ravi Jayakaran is an expert on Participatory Learning and Action, formerly called Participatory Rural Appraisals. Training with Robert Chambers in England introduced him to the ideas of allowing the poor to speak for themselves and of adapting development-planning methodologies so that the poor do the learning. Done properly, the PLA is a helpful tool by which the poor can describe their social systems and survival strategy using their own categories. After watching and listening to the community members as they carry out various exercises, one can develop a fairly clear picture of the community's survival strategy, thus setting the stage for an analysis of capabilities and vulnerabilities. The development goal will then be to build on capacities while reducing vulnerabilities.

From the results of a properly done PLA exercise, the poor can discover how much they really do know, what resources and skills they already have and how resourceful they have been in the past. Helping the poor discover that what they know is valuable goes a long way toward helping them overcome their marred identity. A villager, upon hearing the result of a PLA exercise summarized by village leaders, remarked: "Hey! We're quite smart, aren't we?"

For the last several years Jayakaran has been working to find ways to make PLA results more reflective of the holistic worldview of the people with whom he works. Noting that PLA results tend to focus on material descriptions of village life, and knowing that villagers have a very religious orientation, particularly with regard to cause and effect, Jayakaran wondered if the PLA methodology were not infected with the Western view that the material and spiritual worlds were not connected. He discovered that the PLA methodology was fine; the ones who used it were the source of the problem. Villagers quickly understood that a requested map of village resources was meant to contain only things that can be seen and, being respectful of the educated development promoters, simply edited out the spiritual side of their story.

The PLA tends to be a problem-solving methodology of great power. What it misses, when used in the traditional way, is the things that work, that create energy, that solve problems in the community. Appreciative Inquiry is a newer development-planning tool that seeks to fill this gap. The chapter by Sarone Ole Sena and Dirk Booy summarizes their experience in Tanzania using this new tool.

Appreciative Inquiry stands in contrast to the problem-solving framework of most development-planning methodologies. Instead of looking for what is wrong or missing and developing problem-solving responses, Appreciative Inquiry looks for what is working, successful and life-giving and attempts to see additional possibilities. The belief is that an organization's single-minded "commitment to a problem-solving view of the world acts as a primary constraint on its imagination and contribution to knowledge."[6] The two frameworks can be contrasted in the following way:

	Problem solving	Appreciative Inquiry
Underlying assumptions	Organizing is a problem to be solved.	Organizing is a mystery to be embraced.
Focus	Search for problems	Search for possibilities
Planning metaphor	A problem-solving tree	A possibility tree
Methods	Identify the problems What are the "felt needs"? Analysis of causes Analysis of possible solutions Action planning	Valuing the best What exists that is good? Envisioning what might be Dialoguing about what should be Innovating what will be

Figure 4: Comparing problem solving to Appreciative Inquiry.

In essence, Appreciative Inquiry is more than a method, it is a way of viewing the world. "It is an intentional posture of continuous affirmation of life, of joy, of beauty, of excellence, of innovation."[7] This should remind us of Paul's admonition in Philippians 4:8–9:

> Finally, beloved, whatever is true, whatever is honorable, whatever is just, whatever is pure, whatever is pleasing, whatever is commendable, if there is any excellence and if there is anything worthy of praise, think about these things. Keep on doing the things that you have learned and received and heard and seen in me, and the God of peace will be with you.

The underlying theological frame is that God has created a good and life-giving social world and that wherever we find good in our world, we see evidence of God's work and gifts. The biblical story is the account of God's project to restore the lives of individuals and communities, marred by sin, so that they can be good, just and peaceful once again. An appreciative perspective encourages transformational development promoters to find God's redemptive work in the life of the community, and within themselves, and to seek to become more intentionally part of it. At a more personal level, the appreciative frame also fits the gospel account: in spite of our sin, God looks through our brokenness and, recognizing God's image in us, works to restore that image in its fullness.

The third chapter on development methodologies, written by Elnora Avarientos, Joy Alvarez and Thomas McAlpine, summarizes work being done in the Philippines and in some Latin American countries. The authors report on a new and very different way in which communities use the Bible as a tool for reflection and a source of inspiration. The frame for this use of the Bible goes something like this.

If we think of development as the convergence of several stories, the story of the community joining with the story of the development promoter (and the story of his or her development agency), we must also acknowledge that God has been and is at work in both stories, and that God offers to both a better future story.

The Bible is the only book that Christians believe stands in a privileged position over every human being and every human story. Hans-Ruedi Weber tells the story of a village woman in East Africa who walked around her village carrying a Bible. "Why always the Bible?" her neighbors asked teasingly. "There are lots of other books you could read." Speaking with authority, the woman replied, "Yes, of course there are many books which I could read. But there is only one book which reads me."[8]

In order for the biblical story to be what I have just described, we must take note of some important conditions in terms of how the biblical story is used. The "study, preach and teach" framework of the expository preacher or the theological teacher is an "outside-in" methodology, in which experts provide the knowledge that the non-experts do not have.[9] Like "go and tell" Christian witness, this contradicts the principles of local ownership, local direction and the idea that the responsibility for development, including spiritual development, belongs to the people and not to us. The challenge is to find ways of using the Bible in human and social transformation that place the responsibility for asking questions and seeking answers within the community itself.

One way to do this is to avoid using the biblical text as we would a text-book. We must learn to go beyond studying the Bible solely to report what we have learned to others, since this is speaking for the text. We need to be willing to go beyond studying the Bible to select what we think is useful for what we want to do, since this is using and, almost certainly, limiting the text. When we stand outside the text and look into it as a resource from which we pick and choose, we put ourselves above the text. This stance is exemplified both by historical criticism and by those who favor proof-texting as a tool of persuasion. The village woman in East Africa is right. We must live within the text, allowing it to read us, to examine us, to bring life to us, perhaps even personally to encounter us. We must learn, and the people with whom we work must learn, to use the biblical text as an interpretive lens and as a possible meeting place with God. This is what the staff in the Philippines has been pursuing with Scripture Search, and what staff members have been testing with the Lumko Seven Steps approach in Latin America.

Technical areas of development

The book then moves to two chapters that look at technical issues in development: David Befus on micro-enterprise development and Daniel Ole Shani on urban community organizing in Mauritania.

David Befus has a long and successful track record in micro-enterprise development, first with Opportunity International and then with World Vision. In World Vision, David adapted the proven principles of micro-enterprise development as a stand-alone ministry and worked with countries in Latin America to graft these principles into area development programs. His chapter outlines his vision, describes how he sees this fitting into Christian development work and declares the demands that sustainable micro-enterprise development makes on the Christian NGO.

Many of the people in the Muslim desert nation of Mauritania live around the capital city of Nouakchott. Daniel Ole Shani's chapter describes how former nomads, struggling to adapt to an urban setting, responded to community organizing in wonderful and transforming ways. His chapter is a good example of how community organizing, without a conflictive, politicizing bias, can result in building community where it does not already exist.

Frontiers

The final two chapters sketch possible frontiers for the practice of transformational development: Siobhan O'Reilly describes field research on the potential for reconciliation and peace-building in area development programs. Corina Villacorta describes academic research that explores the possibility, or even the demand, that community development practitioners overcome their bias against the private sector and begin to seek common ground.

While learning about World Vision's participative, community-based approach to area development programming, Siobhan O'Reilly began to wonder if the commitment to the whole community participating and working together might not represent a potential for healing the divisions between groups in the community, and also result in a bias within the community against future conflict. With a grant from the U.K. government, O'Reilly did field research in India and Africa. Her chapter presents her work, with enough validation of her hypothesis to warrant future study.

Corina Villacorta describes her study on the relationship between the NGO world and the private sector. She challenges the NGO development community to set aside its tendency to see the private sector as uniformly being part of the poverty problem, and to move to a more constructive stance. The private sector is the world the poor need to learn to participate in if they are to survive globalization, and the private sector must be given a chance to respond to the call toward greater social responsibility.

Summing up

Working with the Poor concludes with a chapter by Beris Gwynne that provides us with some learnings that resulted from the presentations and discussions held in Austria. Gwynne was the only person invited to Bad Ischl who was not asked to write a paper, and so she became a natural target for the decision about who should write the summary chapter.

As the editor of this book, I am deeply grateful to all my friends who participated in this learning process. Each learned a lot from the far-from-simple exercise of writing up his or her experience. And each learned a lot from one another as we listened and discussed. We are grateful to Sarone Ole Sena and Dirk Booy for leading an "appreciative" exercise at the conclusion of each discussion: What did you like? What excited you? What are you going to appropriate for your own work?

Now it's your turn to participate in this learning exercise. We offer these chapters not as the final work but simply as an experience. Read them

xxii   BRYANT L. MYERS

alongside your own experience. Listen to your mind and heart. Take what helps you, and pass over what does not.

Notes

[1] Much of what immediately follows is taken from *Walking With the Poor* (Maryknoll, N.Y.: Orbis Books, 1999).

[2] Lesslie Newbigin, *The Gospel in a Pluralist Society* (Geneva: WCC, 1989).

[3] Paul G. Hiebert, "The Flaw of the Excluded Middle." *Missiology* 10, no. 1 (1982): 35–47.

[4] Having noted the holism in the biblical worldview and the fact that most traditional worldviews are holistic is not to say that the biblical worldview is animistic. The biblical and animistic worldviews are quite different. There is only one God in the biblical worldview, and spiritual beings are solely part of the created order and are also fallen, just like human beings.

[5] Bruce Bradshaw, *Bridging the Gap* (Monrovia, Calif.: MARC, 1993).

[6] David L. Cooperrider and Suresh Srivastva, "Appreciative Inquiry in Organizational Life," *Research in Organizational Change and Development* 1 (1987), 129.

[7] Scott Johnson and James D. Ludema, *Partnering to Build and Measure Organizational Capacity: Lessons from NGOs around the World* (Grand Rapids, Mich.: Christian Reformed World Relief Committee, 1997), 72.

[8] Hans-Ruedi Weber, *The Book That Reads Me* (Geneva: WCC 1995).

[9] I am not implying that expository preachers or theological teachers are using inappropriate methods. Exposition and formal teaching methods are ideal for church and classroom settings. I am only trying to say that community development is very different, and thus makes different requirements of us when it comes to using the Bible.

PART ONE

FRAMEWORK

1

An Alternate Reading of Poverty

Jayakumar Christian

Before we take a fresh look at models of transformational initiatives among the poor, it is important for us to examine our understanding of poverty. Our understanding of the poor and their relationships must shape our models of transformation. How do we understand the people we seek to serve—the poor? What is the context of our transformational initiatives?

Poverty continues to defy simplistic descriptions, definitions and easy solutions. It continues to raise very uncomfortable questions for our continued reflection and response.

Essentially, poverty is about relationships. It is a flesh-and-blood experience of a people within their day-to-day relationships. Within these relationships, the poor experience deprivation, powerlessness, physical isolation, economic poverty and all other characteristics of poverty. This chapter seeks to examine the many dimensions of this relationship. It focuses on the nature and causes of chronic intergenerational poverty. The author hopes that this alternative reading of poverty will provide some defining parameters for constructing the next-generation paradigm of transformation.

POVERTY—CAPTIVITY WITHIN THE GOD COMPLEXES OF THE POWERFUL

Any serious student of poverty is immediately confronted with the fact that all is not well with relationships in poverty situations. Even the "perfect social harmony" of the powerful is not without its cracks and flaws. For poverty is about a powerful minority, "less numerous, [which] perform[s] all political functions, monopolize[s] power and enjoy[s] the advantages that power brings" (Curtis 1981, 332). These powerful seek to play god in the lives of the poor, reinforcing each other to form a "god complex." To play god in the lives of the vulnerable is essentially an expression of the inherent ability of humans to be evil.

The nature of god complexes

Let me explain the term *god complex*. In poverty situations, the term refers to those who:

- seek to absolutize themselves.
- base their power on what Max Weber calls the "eternal yesterday" (Curtis 1981, 427) to influence the "eternal tomorrows" of the poor.
- seek to influence areas of the life of the poor that are beyond their particular scope of influence (Wrong 1979, 250). Among commercial sex workers, for example, the landlord may go beyond the money-lender role to act as the "protector" of the girls in the community, shielding them from the local police and the political powers. The commercial sex workers, however, have to buy this "protection." The landlord is going beyond his specific scope of influence.
- within poverty situations claim immutability. They operate under the assumption that they will never experience "power deflation,"[1] and their power can never be challenged.
- work in conjunction with others to keep the poor powerless, making it a "complex." It is the interplay of several power holders that keeps the poor powerless.

This tendency to absolutize power, influence eternal tomorrows, over-flow scope-specific influence, claim immutability and fear power deflation are traits that are normally attributed to gods. In poverty situations the powerful seek to play the role of god in the lives of the poor.

Walter Wink's description of the "domination system" in his book *Un-masking the Powers* parallels the description of the god complexes in poverty relationships (Wink 1992).[2] Wink describes the "domination system" as a system that:

- demands that the world value power as an end in itself;
- requires society to become more like itself;
- acquires a sense of independence "beyond human control";
- assumes an identity of its own; and
- wounds the soul of its subjects (Wink 1992, 54, 40, 41, 41, 101).

These god complexes hold the poor captive. They feel threatened with any transformational initiative that undermines their foundations. They operate through people, systems and structures (Liddle 1992, 795). Religious systems, mass media, law, government policies and people in power-ful positions all serve to reinforce the god complexes that keep the poor poor.

God complexes also have an ideological center, an inner reality that governs and holds together the structures, systems and people. This inner reality provides the logic for the structures and systems, and offers interpretations on ultimate values for life, events and processes. For example, the media, apart from marketing products passionately, also aggressively promote a particular interpretation of life's ultimate values. Since these ideological centers deal with ultimate values, I refer to them as "inner spiritualities" or "spiritual interiorities." Structures and systems are inextricably rooted in these spiritual interiorities. They form the "spirituality" of the various economic, social, political, bureaucratic and religious structures and systems. Therefore, apart from structure, systems and people, there is the "interiority of earthly institutions or structures or systems" (Wink 1992, 77). These inner spiritualities provide that underlying "spiritual dimension in the victimization of the poor and the power accruing activity of the systems" (Linthicum 1991, 19).

So god complexes are clusters of power (social, economic, bureaucratic, political and religious) within the domain of poverty relationships that absolutize themselves to keep the poor powerless. These god complexes hold the poor captive.

Redefining who rules

If poverty is about the god complexes of the non-poor and related structures, systems, people and spiritual interiorities, then our transformational initiatives must seek to reverse these god complexes. Transformation is about challenging the god complexes that cause the human spirit to bow down to any other than its Creator. This challenge must involve encounters with persons, structures, systems and spiritual interiorities that perpetuate the god complexes. Transformation is more than a bundle of successful "sustainable" programs—it is an encounter of conflicting spiritualities.

If transformational initiatives must challenge god complexes within poverty situations, then establishing the kingdom of God must be a valid alternative. God's kingdom does not co-exist with other kingdoms and god complexes. The kingdom of God is that radical alternative to oppressive god complexes. Proclaiming the absolute nature of the King of the kingdom of God in the face of these god complexes is the most radical of all options. The kingdom of God challenges all other initiatives that seek to absolutize themselves in the lives of the poor. If we are to challenge the god complexes, then the kingdom of God is not peripheral to our models of transformation—it is the core.

Establishing God's rule will also involve an encounter at the spirituality level and will challenge our flawed understanding of power. It is important to communicate the kingdom's understanding that all power belongs to God (Ps. 62).

This understanding of poverty and consequent model of transformational response to the poor makes our involvement more than simple development work. It is a prophetic ministry of a dependent community—challenging the god complexes.

Some questions for our consideration

- Do our transformational initiatives consistently express the reign of God among us?
- Are we enabling communities to discover and live under the reign of God?
- Are we seeking to reverse the god complexes that keep the poor poor?
- Do we tend to become a god complex ourselves over the poor?
- Do our development teams believe and express a redefined understanding of power—power as defined by the Word?
- Do we train our teams to understand and analyze the structure, systems, people, values and spiritual interiorities that characterize a god complex?
- Do our definitions of sustainability and empowerment include equipping the poor to deal with structure, systems, people, values and spiritual interiorities?

POVERTY—THE RESULT OF BROKEN RELATIONSHIPS

Another important mark of poverty situations is broken relationships. The poor are excluded from the mainstream of society, and their sense of community is marred.

Exclusion from the mainstream

First, let us examine the exclusion of the poor from the mainstream of society. It is a "systematic process of disempowerment" (Friedmann 1992, 30), excluding the poor from the economic, political, social, bureaucratic and religious mainstream of society. It is also a selective process.

This exclusion of the poor is rooted in the world's rejection of the wisdom of the poor as not worthy of any attention. As Len Doyal and Ian Gough rightly point out, the voice of the poor is regarded as "damaged goods" by the powerful—blemished either by ignorance or self-interest, consequently giving way to abuses of power (1991, 11).

The poor also exclude themselves by not participating in social and political processes. The poor do not speak up; they may even decline to sit down with the powerful. Weak, powerless and isolated, they are often reluctant to push themselves forward (Chambers 1988, 18).

Society uses different social systems to exclude the poor. The legal system is probably the most commonly used tool in this process. The "legality" of economic systems excludes the poor. Legality becomes a privilege available only to those with political and economic power; those excluded—the poor—have no alternative but illegality (Llosa 1989, xii).

Apart from legal systems, the education system is also designed to ensure intergenerational exclusion of the poor from the mainstream. Poor children are excluded from this system, thus creating the future poor. Arguing that curriculum development is always both political and pedagogical, Paulo Freire concludes:

> It is the very structures of society that create a serious set of barriers and difficulties, some in solidarity with others, that result in enormous obstacles for the children of subordinate classes to come to school (Freire 1993, 30).

Fragmentation of community

Apart from excluding the poor from the mainstream, the sense of community among the poor is always under attack. For the poor, being a community is an integral part of who they are—their basic unit and their survival mechanism. The powerful always threaten the sense of community in poverty situations.

Power threatens community; it is divisive. When power encounters poverty, the community base is eroded. As Sik Hung Ng points out, power breeds conflict. Humans oppose humans in the struggle to attain, share or influence power. "Power is, therefore, divisive and leads to antagonism and conflict" (Ng 1980, 85).

The poor's response to exploitative expressions of power also results in the disintegration of the community. They either "exit," or express "loyalty" or "voice" their response (Chambers 1983, 142, 143). Each of these fragments the community further.

The very nature of power, the role of the elite and the response of the poor all contribute toward eroding the community base.

Redefining community

If poverty is about broken relationships—exclusion from society's mainstream and the fragmentation of community—then our transformational initiatives must result in rebuilding community. We must move beyond community organizing to something more radical and fundamental.

The Christian faith offers the most radical of responses to these situations, namely, the formation of covenantal communities. The covenantal community that the Christian faith offers is a community of unequals with trust, celebration and redemption as its chief characteristics. I suggest that creating covenant communities (patterned after Yahweh's covenant with Creation) must be an integral part of our response, both among the poor and between the poor and the non-poor.

Jesus rebuilt community by challenging the very lines that divided people. He further made those lines a religious issue about which God was deeply concerned. While issue-based community organization techniques exploit numbers and mobilize people around issues, covenantal communities deal with issues without reducing the poor to mere numbers. Personhood is valued; diversity is celebrated and not exploited. Rebuilding relationships demands investing in relationships. A key question for us, therefore, is this: Have our models of transformation enabled us to invest in relationships and build covenantal communities that do not gloss over issues but instead create celebrating communities?

Some questions for our consideration

- Do our teams express a true sense of community—a covenantal community?
- Do we have a way of being a reconciled team ourselves?
- Do we have a way of healing each other so we can become agents of healing rather than multiplying hurt?
- Do our definitions of and strategies for sustainability, empowerment and community organization include building covenantal communities—communities among the poor as well as between the poor and the non-poor?
- Do we facilitate "win-win" relationships within poverty situations?
- Do our offices and centers become places for healing broken relationships?

POVERTY—THE RESULT OF HOPELESSNESS AND DISTORTED HISTORY

It is impossible to understand intergenerational poverty without raising the question of time. Deep-seated hopelessness in poverty situations demands our attention. Unfortunately, hope and hopelessness are often thought of as belonging to the realm of the future. Human experience, however, suggests that hope and hopelessness are more than a state of mind or a thing of the future. Hope and hopelessness shape the powerlessness of the marginalized today.

Hopelessness is today's experience

First, hopelessness prevents meaningful action today. It results in disinterested action, lack of desire for change and low aspirations. This cycle of hopelessness and lack of interest in changing the present pushes the marginalized into extreme powerlessness. Hopelessness is more than a future thing; it shapes the present and perpetuates powerlessness.

Second, powerlessness is vicious. Powerlessness destroys hope today. Powerlessness and hopelessness reinforce each other to hold the poor in permanent captivity within a vicious cycle of deprivation. Further, the powerful do everything to crush any glimmer of hope among the poor, since hope among the poor is a threat to the powerful. Hopelessness causes powerlessness, and powerlessness destroys hope. This vicious circle of hopelessness and powerlessness among the poor destroys the very energy needed to live.

Hopelessness is a product of history

Hopelessness is rooted in the history of a people. The future is shaped in a laboratory called history. History is an important dimension for understanding poverty and hopelessness in poverty situations. The relationship between history and poverty is not a new arena in poverty studies.[3] There are several ways in which different forces within a people's history have an impact on their present. I focus here intentionally on *interpreted-remembered* and *shared* aspects of history at the *micro-level* that shape poverty relationships.[4]

History is distorted in many ways. Let me highlight a few ways in which history is distorted as it relates to the powerlessness of the poor.

First, the *substance* of remembered and interpreted history tends to marginalize the poor, the girl child and women. The powerful not only exercise power but also set the agenda and rules for the exercise of power within poverty relationships. Marvin Olsen in *Power in Modern Societies* (Olsen and Marger 1993) calls this form of power that sets the agenda and rules "meta power." Meta power is the ability to "shape the aggregate action and interaction possibilities of those involved in the situation" (ibid., 36). The powerful shape the rules for relationships and define the wants of the poor. They ascribe meaning to life situations, which then shape poverty relationships.

Second, the *process* of history-making also becomes a source of powerlessness. While it is true all humans are free to make history, in reality some humans are much freer than others to do so. In the bargain, those who "do not make history . . . tend increasingly to become the utensils of history-makers as well as mere objects of history" (Wright 1993). In this major venture of the powerful to write and rewrite history, the powerless become mere objects. Therefore, the history-making process itself is a source of powerlessness for the poor.

Third, the *opportunity* to read reality is also curtailed by the powerful. Paulo Freire defined literacy as the "reading of the world," and concluded that much of the education system does not enable the poor to read their own world (Freire 1993). The poor read the world through the lens that the powerful have lent them. In his famous conscientization strategy for liberation from oppression, Freire advocates that "each man [must] win back his right to *say his own word, to name the world*" (Freire 1990, 13). Years of intergenerational poverty seriously cramp the ability of the poor to even name their reality. It is a distorted reading of reality and history—a reading from the perspective of the powerful.

Finally, the socioeconomic *cost* of these distortions of history is very high for the poor. When the poor become mere tools in the hands of history-makers, the rest of their life also gets defined by the "station" assigned to them in the histories written by the powerful. Even rules for life situations and relationships are molded by history.

Redefining history

For a community characterized by hopelessness and shaped by distorted histories, the kingdom of God provides a liberating alternative. As followers of the Lord Jesus Christ we can reread distorted history with God as the point of reference. This becomes an alternative perspective to reading the history provided by the powerful. It is an alternative to a world that constantly tells the poor that even God has forsaken their communities and families.

This rereading of history must affirm that God is active and interested in the history of the poor. This rereading of history must also recognize that history is not the savior; salvation comes from the Lord of history. Rereading history is more than rewriting it from the poor's perspective. Neither the victor nor the vanquished is the valid starting point for the rereading project. History written from the perspective of the powerless will only mean reversing the format, not transforming history. The challenge is to read history while affirming that God is active in the histories of people.

Rereading history while affirming God's action in history opens up the possibility for the powerless to imagine the future anew. It affirms that the future need no longer be a mere extension of distorted versions of history. The new future need not be out of bounds to the poor. The marginalized, who have constantly been denied this history-making role and have become tools in the hands of the world's history-makers, now have a new opportunity to imagine a future characterized by hope.

Imagining a new future is a ministry of "prophetic imagination." This prophetic imagination must precede any concrete response (Brueggemann 1978, 45). It is a response that "is empowering the poor in a manner which encourages and enables them to take the *long view*, to enhance and not degrade resources" (Chambers 1991, 5, emphasis added). Only then can the poor dream of a new future.

In this task of imagining a new future, the prophet of God provides leadership. It is the vocation of the prophet to keep alive the ministry of imagination and hope and to provide a liberating alternative to what has been for generations thought of as the only thinkable reading of history and reality, that of the powerful (Brueggemann 1978, 45).

Some questions for our consideration

- Do we consciously enable the poor to see God in their history, even as we facilitate the use of our analytical tools (participatory learning and action, dream mapping and so on)?
- Do we consciously challenge the world's message/disinformation that God is not involved in the histories of the poor?
- Do our teams function in a way that affirms what God has done and is doing among our colleagues?
- Do our definitions and strategies for sustainability and empowerment include equipping the poor to reread their history and reality so they can imagine a new future?
- Do our transformational initiatives minister hope in the midst of despair?
- Do our teams initiate hope-based action?

POVERTY—RESULT OF MARRED IDENTITY OF THE POOR

Poverty is about personhood and identity. By marring identity the powerful seek to inflict permanent damage to the poor. Let us examine a few ways by which the poor's identity is manipulated and marred.

The process of marring

First, flawed social norms and a people's worldview are used to mar the identity of the poor. In the Indian context, the caste system is the mold used for shaping social norms. In various cultures, religion and traditions have served as major tools to reinforce these norms. For example, a community's caste traditions, accompanied by fear of shame, perpetuate intergenerational temple prostitution in parts of India.[5] When traditions, fear of shame and marred identity combine, powerlessness is the product. The powerless have no option but to submit.

Second, years of marginalization mar the identity of the poor. The fact that girls are born with a distinct social disadvantage leaves a negative imprint on their minds. This is more than stunting of their aspirations and awareness. It also affects the poor's ability to reflect critically and analyze their situation. Years of exploitation have reduced the marginalized to dull, submissive living objects. Their perpetual exploitation freezes their minds. Consequently, self-image and identity are shaped by the hurt and pain that the poor carry in their minds. Dullness of the mind along with hurt and pain serve to perpetuate powerlessness among the poor.

Third, the powerful intentionally reduce the poor to mere objects.

> In their unrestrained eagerness to possess, the oppressors develop the conviction that it is possible for them to transform everything into objects of their purchasing power; . . . for the oppressors, what is worthwhile is to have more—always more—even at the cost of the oppressed having less or having nothing. For them, *to be is to have* and to be the class of the "haves" (Freire 1990, 44).

The poor become less than human in the process, their identity defined by the mere object status assigned to them (Freire 1990, 20, 55).

Fourth, marring the poor's identity is a prelude to further exploitation. It seems natural that any exploitation and oppression must deal with the question of the identity of the oppressed. Once the oppressor ascribes a "low identity" to the poor, then all consequent acts become "legitimate" behavior. For example, the girl child becomes "unwanted" before she is exploited by the oppressor. The wives of the landless become "property" before the landlord abuses them sexually. The landless become debtors before they are abused and humiliated by the moneylender.

To summarize, powerlessness is a product of the poor's marred identity. Through oppressive social norms, stunting of the mind, retarding reflective ability and reducing the poor to mere objects, society mars the identity of the poor.

Redefining identity

Transformational initiatives must address issues of identity; they should facilitate clarifying the identity of the poor. Our point of reference for this process of identity clarification is the knowledge that all are made in the image of God. Further, this image is a gift from God; the image of God is not earned. Quality standards such as empowerment and sustainability need redefinition as well, if they are to deal with the issue of marred identity.

Some questions for our consideration

- Do we relate with the poor in a way that consistently and consciously affirms that the poor are made in the image of God?
- Do we affirm or mar the identity of our staff or members of our team?
- Do we equip our staff to rightly divide the Word, teach from the Word, and link the Word to the context?

- Do our definitions and strategies for sustainability and empowerment include clarifying the identity of the poor?
- Do our transformational initiatives challenge the lie that the world promotes, namely, that the poor are not made in the image of God?

POVERTY—THE RESULT OF INADEQUACIE IN A PEOPLE'S WORLDVIEW

Poverty is a much broader concept than sociopolitics and economics. A survey of various development theories suggests that the roots of poverty can be traced to a people's worldview. This is not a simple ethnocentric statement; it is an acknowledgment that a people's worldview is a powerful tool for perpetuating chronic poverty. Development ethicists[6] and community psychologists are calling development practitioners to consider seriously worldview-related issues (Rappaport 1987, 139–42).

Worldview is a practical tool within the culture of a people (Kearney 1984, 66). Worldview serves as a framework to explain, evaluate, validate, prioritize commitments, interpret, integrate and adapt to various realities and pressures of life (Kraft 1989, 183).

Let me illustrate the role of worldview in perpetuating poverty by examining one theme in popular Hinduism. (I use Hinduism only as a case in point for this analysis. All cultures have their elements of fallenness).

Karma (willed activity, reaping the result of one's past deeds) is probably the most frequently studied of all beliefs of the Hindu poor. The Upanishads[7] summarize well the underlying philosophical basis of karma:

> By the holy deeds, he becomes holy; by sinful ones, sinful. It is for this reason that they say that a person consists merely of desires (*kama*); as his desire is, so his will (*kratuh*); as his will is, so his deed (karma); as his deed is, so his evolution (quotation from Upanishads iv, 4,2, in Prabhu 1940, 20).

The karma of a person affects the person's physical existence now—size, shape, color, appearance and so on. Karma also affects the "social position, including the class or caste into which we are born. It even affects whether we are born as humans or as some lower or higher form of life" (Reichenbach 1990, 51).

Karma is not a mechanical principle but a spiritual necessity. It is the embodiment of the mind and will of God. God is its supervisor. . . . Justice is an attribute of God (Radhakrishnan 1927, 53).

The belief in the migration of the soul (*samsara*) further intensifies the negative effects of the karma theory. Average Hindus dread future births and deaths since they reckon that the soul has to go through several million births and deaths with no necessary assurance of progress (Appasamy 1942, 115–20).

Karma and poverty

In poverty situations worldview assumptions based on karma hold several negative implications for the poor. Karma theory interprets the "person-group" aspect of society in terms of the results of past karma. Karma classifies society into two categories—those whose karma is good and others, like the poor, whose karma is bad. Among the non-poor this karma-based understanding of person-group enables them to believe that the poor are paying for their bad deeds of the past, that poverty is the result of the bad karma of the poor. The non-poor believe their wealth, irrespective of how it is acquired, is the fruit of their good karma.

Therefore, in a community where karma is a defining worldview, poverty becomes a natural consequence. Such cause-effect relationships can be traced in all poverty situations. Poverty is a worldview issue.

Redefining worldviews

Poverty challenges cannot be adequately responded to if we do not confront the worldview inadequacies of the people involved. A worldview-level understanding of the causes of poverty demands going beyond the traditional "being culturally sensitive" stance. We need tools to analyze worldview-level inadequacies, both among the poor and the non-poor. Transformational initiatives must intentionally pursue worldview-level encounters.

This critique of worldview-level inadequacies almost immediately calls for a reference point that can guide the critique and serve as the alternate point of view. For followers of Jesus Christ, this must necessarily be the Word of God. We must become the hermeneutical community who will study the Word of God in context, who will provide leadership in this process of confronting poverty at the worldview level.

Some questions for our consideration

- Do we equip our staff teams and the communities with which we work to analyze the worldview of the poor and the non-poor in poverty situations?
- Do our baselines include gathering and analyzing data related to the community's worldview?
- Do we know how to analyze our own worldview themes and challenge inadequacies on the basis of the Word?

- Do our sustainability and empowerment definitions and strategies include challenging sensitively the meaning ascribed by the community to various aspects of reality that perpetuate poverty?
- Do our programs affirm those aspects of culture and worldview that do not perpetuate poverty, but instead affirm values that are consistent for creating a world that does not tolerate poverty?
- Do we develop and use various means within programs to address worldview inadequacies?
- Do we consciously develop the skill of the staff teams rightly to divide the Word and allow the Word to critique the community's worldviews, as well as our own?

POVERTY—THE RESULT OF EXPLOITATION BY PRINCIPALITIES AND POWERS

Any effort to understand the meaning of poverty must grapple with yet another dimension of reality, namely, the role of principalities and powers in poverty situations.

Mission anthropologist Paul Hiebert's analysis of the different perceptions of reality and the "excluded middle" triggered several reevaluations of traditional perceptions of the causes of poverty. According to Hiebert, the influence of Enlightenment thinking, dualism and a mechanistic perception of reality influenced mission thinking. Consequently, the dualistic view of reality excluded important dimensions of reality, including the middle tier. Hiebert describes this middle level as including

> beings [which] are forces that cannot be directly perceived but thought to exist on this earth. These include spirits, ghosts, ancestors, demons, and earthly gods and goddesses who live in trees, rivers, hills and villages. These live not in some other world or time, but are inhabitants with humans and animals of this world and time. . . . This level also includes supernatural forces such as manna, planetary influences, evil eyes and the powers of magic, sorcery and witchcraft (1982, 41).

Most Christian missions are built on a fragmented and dualistic perception of reality. On the other hand, for the Hindu poor, all of life is directly or indirectly related to the work of spiritual power: sickness, a failed business and social ostracism can all be explained in terms of spiritual power working against the poor. Demons, shamans, witch doctors and gods mediate this spiritual power.

Poverty is not only rooted in the fall of humans but is also a result of the present working of the Evil One. Missiologists and grassroots practitioners affirm that "behind all poverty is the devil . . . [and] the ultimate cause of poverty is the devil himself" (Duncan 1990, 9). Therefore, authentic and sustainable involvement among the poor will involve confrontation with the powers of the Evil One. "The Son of God was revealed for this purpose, to destroy the works of the devil" (1 John 3:8).

Through the years there have been several debates on the identity of the cosmic powers.[8] A common view is that God created the powers, and they were meant to serve God's purposes. However, after the Fall the powers were set against God's purposes and were particularly directed against God's creation. "Now they are 'behaving' as though they were the ultimate ground of being" (Mouw 1976, 89). The powers seek to absolutize themselves. They are enemies of Christ (Ps. 110:1, Eph. 6:11–12, 16; 2:2; 4:27; Arnold 1989, 56). References to the powers also indicate that there is a plurality of powers (Mouw 1976, 86). The powers belong to the kingdom of Satan (Kraft 1992, 19) and wield control over people. I have opted to understand principalities and powers as personal beings (Arnold 1992, 77) and forces (Arnold 1988, 44–51) that have a dominating influence on persons, social organizations and groups (Kraft 1992, 19), and structures.

Poverty, principalities and powers

There are several ways in which the Devil and his forces influence persons. Let me confine myself to the role of the principalities and powers in poverty situations.

First, the powers reinforce various deceptions that have roots in a people's belief system. They blind the mind (2 Cor. 4:4). The poor are made to believe that their *varna* (each of the four original castes of Hindu society) and their duty (*sav-dharma*) define their identity. The Devil and his forces are great deceivers (2 Tim. 2:26; Gal. 4:3; Eph. 2:12). They keep the poor enslaved, captive and under deception about their role in society, their place in the hierarchy of *varnas* and their place in God's presence (Arnold 1992, 93). The deception these powers perpetuate to keep the poor powerless is well illustrated by the experiences of poor communities. Through these deceptions the prince of the power of the air (Eph. 2:2) seeks to keep the poor powerless. Often these deceptions lead people away from God. As Heinrich Schlier suggests, it is the nature of these powers to "present and interpret everything in the universe which they dominate in their own light and in their own way" (Schlier 1961, 32).

Second, the principalities and powers attack the body through disease (Matt. 9:32, 33; Luke 13:16; 2 Cor. 12:7). This is probably why churches that minister to the health and physical well-being of their members attract the poor. The poor and the non-poor alike are vulnerable to exploitation by the principalities and powers in this area. For the poor, however, sickness has greater socioeconomic costs. It pushes them to the edge of survival. It creates dependence on moneylenders, high debts, absence from work and other negative economic implications. They become dependent on village priests and witchcraft, which in turn drain the poor financially.

Third, the role of the powers in influencing people through compulsive dependence on certain habits is also well known. The cost of maintaining compulsive behaviors is high and erodes the poor's financial base. The poor do not have the same options that the non-poor have. These habits and destructive options spell vulnerability and powerlessness for the poor, who already grapple with economic crises, and result in perpetual socioeconomic captivity of households (Schlier 1961, 33).

Fourth, the Devil attacks relationships that were meant to serve as positive agents in shaping identities. He sows seeds of enmity between people and keeps the poor, who are already on the fringe of society, divided. While not blaming the Devil for all the disunity in the community, it is necessary to recognize that unity and brotherhood are not the Devil's cup of tea. Marred relationships are a mark of abiding in death (1 John 3:14), while unity and brotherhood are a sign of life.

Fifth, the Devil also exploits curses that people cast on each other. "A curse is the invocation of the power of Satan or of God to affect negatively the person or thing at which the curse is directed" (Kraft 1992, 75). Very often, the effects of curses on the poor have serious socioeconomic costs (e.g., the Bhils in western India define themselves as "cursed people"—cursed by God before Creation).

Sixth, cosmic principalities and powers seek to control the will of the poor. "The ultimate aim of the enemy is not simply to control people's minds but to get at their wills" (Kraft 1990, 272). By capturing a person's will, the Devil seeks to influence choices in life. Within popular Hinduism karma, *samsara* (the cyclical understanding of time and events) and other such beliefs aid the Devil. Consequently, hopelessness and powerlessness set in.

Seventh, the Devil and his forces seek to cripple the identities (Kraft 1992, 82) of persons involved in poverty relationships. The principalities and powers deceive the poor into believing they are not made in the image of God. This lie is easier to sell when the poor believe God has forsaken them. The poor "feel nonexistent, valueless, humiliated [and believe that they] . . . are stupid, ignorant people who know nothing . . . like oxen who know nothing" (Wink 1992, 101). In this context powerlessness is an issue of identity and reinforced by cosmic powers (Wink 1992, 103). Often, the Devil feeds on the "spiritual garbage" (Kraft 1990, 276) in the person and the community, abusing marred identities, hurt from broken relationships and the pain of captivity to a harsh religious belief system. The principalities and powers play a crucial role in intensifying the powerlessness imposed by society on the poor, reinforcing oppression and carrying it to its logical end of marring the poor's will and identity.

Apart from influencing persons involved in poverty relationships, the principalities and powers also affect the context within which these relationships take place. The term *context* here refers to structures and systems, which are very much a part of any poverty situation. There has been much debate on the role of the powers in relation to the structures and systems.[9]

There are four aspects to the role of principalities and powers vis-à-vis structures that I would like to consider here. The powers:

1. influence structures and systems through people. They manipulate a culture's social, political, economic, religious and even artistic subsystems by acting through individuals (Wagner and Pennoyer 1990, 256).
2. shape the interiority of structures and systems. This interiority is not a reference to the powers, as Wink suggests, but the powers influence these interiorities. The powers ensure that relative powers always seek to absolutize themselves (become god complexes), socioeconomically and politically exclude the poor, cause the community to become non-community, mar the identity of the poor and so on.
3. exploit belief systems and worldviews, and manipulate the context of poverty relationships (1 Cor. 8:4, 5; 10:19–20; Arnold 1992, 94). However, the powers also exploit any form of idolatry, irrespective of which religious system nurtures it.
4. have access to poor families through symbols and articles of significance. The powers empower various symbols and forms within religious systems. These symbols and forms are not as neutral as they appear.

Redefining the role of the principalities and powers

The role of principalities and powers in poverty situations demands that we recognize that transformation is essentially a battle—a battle against principalities and powers. Transformational initiatives must then be an effort to unmask the principalities and powers. We need to confront the Devil and his forces in the context of poverty relationships.

We must pray for our staff members as they confront the Devil. Prayer and fasting must become essential tools for transformational initiatives. The gifts of the Spirit should be used within the context of confronting poverty. The whole armor of God must become the dress code for all those who seek to confront the principalities and powers.

Christian involvement among the poor cannot ignore this aspect of poverty situations. If poverty is the result of the exploitative role of the cosmic powers, there is no way we can be involved in poverty situations without the anointing of the Holy Spirit. We must live in daily obedience to the Holy Spirit. There is a need to be "spiritual" at the core of our response.

Some questions for our consideration

- Do we recognize that our transformational initiatives are a battle with the principalities and powers and that these same initiatives require unmasking the principalities and powers?

- Do we "use" prayer and fasting as tools for social action, going beyond personal spiritual disciplines?
- Do we help our staff recognize and use the gifts of the Spirit as valid development skills?
- Do we require staff members to wear the whole armor of God as their uniform?
- Do we provide prayer cover for front-line staff in the battle? Do we recognize that leadership includes providing prayer cover for staff members and their families?
- Do our definitions and strategies of sustainability and empowerment include communicating the message to the powers that Jesus is Lord?

POVERTY—CAPTIVITY OF THE POOR IN A WEB OF LIES

Throughout the analysis of poverty relationships in this chapter the common theme has been the underlying death and distortion of truth and the perpetuation of lies. Lies are the thread that links the perpetuation of god complexes, the distortion of history, the marring of identity, the fragmentation of relationships, the role of the principalities and powers and the inadequacies in worldview themes. Flawed assumptions and interpretations (lack of truth) that are rooted in religious systems, the worldview of a people and the work of the principalities and powers sustain oppressive relationships.

A helpful image to represent the captivity of the poor in a world of flawed assumptions and interpretations is the idea of a web. In the context of poverty relationships, this web is essentially a web of lies—that social status is divinely sanctioned, that poverty cannot be changed, for example. Both the poor and the non-poor believe these lies and thus ensure perpetuation of the powerlessness of the poor.

Various worldview themes reviewed in this chapter and the principalities and powers that reinforce these themes form the web of lies.[10] It is a web of lies within which the poor are held captive. It is a web of lies that is more than a cognitive level deception. It is a web that affects the lives, attitudes and relationships of the poor. The structures, systems, people, and principalities and powers involved in poverty relationships nurture this web, which is rooted in the worldview of a people. It is seen as an expression of God's justice and believed to be a spiritual necessity. It affirms the status quo.

Redefining truth

If poverty is the captivity of the poor in a web of lies, then the most appropriate response of the church will involve proclaiming the truth. Transformational initiatives must proclaim truth in public places. They must proclaim the truth about the identity of the poor—that they are made in the image of God. Transformation must go beyond the transfer of power to the very redefinition of power. Our work must show that we recognize that we are in the business of communicating truth to the cosmic powers (Eph. 3:8–10). We are involved in the task of proclaiming the Truth that sets us free. This ministry of proclaiming truth within poverty situations is the task of a prophetic community. Transformation must seek to establish truth and righteousness in poverty situations.

Some questions for our consideration

- Do we recognize that we are called to be a prophetic community, to proclaim the truth?
- Do our definitions and strategies include reordering the relationship between truth and power, establishing truth in public life and proclaiming Truth as the basis of all relationships?
- Do we proclaim truth within poverty relationships?
- Do we live and express truth within ourselves? Do we have the strength to challenge the lies that exist in our midst?

What have we learned about poverty?

This chapter suggests that we need to understand poverty holistically before we seek to develop a holistic response to the poor. It suggests broadening the scope of our inquiry into poverty to include examining:

- the captivity of the poor in the god complexes of the non-poor, structures, systems and the cosmic powers;
- the impact of broken relationships (exclusion from the mainstream and the fragmentation of community base);
- the role of hope or hopelessness, as well as distorted interpretations of history;
- the impact of the marred identity of the poor;
- the relationship between poverty and inadequacies in the worldviews of the poor and the non-poor;
- the role of principalities and powers;
- the captivity of the poor in a web of lies.

This chapter also suggests that this perspective about the causes of poverty demands a response that is radically different from our traditional transformational development programs and initiatives. I have suggested that we must reexamine our definitions and strategies for transformational initiatives, empowerment, sustainability and other parameters for our involvement.

Transformational development: Our definitions of transformational development must include initiatives that express the reign of God, create covenantal communities, follow a God who is active and Lord over history in imagining a new future, restore the image of God in the poor, encounter worldview inadequacies, are involved in a spiritual battle with the cosmic powers through the enabling power of the Holy Spirit, and, finally, proclaim the Truth that liberates.

Measurements of sustainability: These measurements must include the impact on structures, systems and people, as well as spiritual interiorities that characterize god complexes, relationships in the community, the role of the poor in society, the identity of the poor, perception among the poor and the non-poor about the histories of the poor, inadequate aspects in worldviews, the role of the principalities and powers, and the role of truth in public life.

Empowerment: The various aspects of poverty examined here also call for a fresh look at our definitions of and strategies for empowerment. Our empowerment strategies must include redefining the very nature of power itself. It is important to examine issue-based community organizational strategies that tend to demonize the powerful and build sacred images around the causes of the powerless. We need to work toward building covenantal communities with both the poor and the non-poor, communities that celebrate diversity without glossing over issues of oppression and exploitation. Empowerment should include challenging the lines that divide the poor, and the poor from the non-poor. Further, empowerment also means equipping the poor to challenge all tendencies to absolutize powers, to exclude the poor from society's mainstream and to divide communities. The poor must be empowered to reread history, affirming God's action in the history of the poor. Empowerment must include equipping the poor to critique their worldview and challenge the principalities and powers and all forces that perpetuate lies in public places.

THREE KEY IMPLICATIONS FOR AN OVERALL APPROACH TO POVERTY

In closing, let me place before you three key implications of this analysis of poverty relationships for an overall approach to poverty.

Our response to the poor must address the whole context of poverty

We must recognize that poverty is about relationships, and goes beyond mere statistics. My analysis suggests there are several key players and factors in any poverty situation. The god complexes need to be addressed, broken relationships need to healed, forces that mar the identity of the poor must be challenged, the lines that divide must be actively ignored, covenantal communities with poor and non-poor must be formed, the cosmic powers need to be unmasked and truth must shape and inform public life. If we are to address poverty adequately, transformation must have an impact on the context of poverty as well. Transformation cannot be merely an event or a series of disconnected events; transformation must address the whole. Transformation has to affect every person involved in any given situation.

Therefore, our focus should be more than just transformation—it should be on initiating *ripples of transformation*—a series of well planned transformations that influence the whole context of poverty, the poor and the non-poor, the structures, systems, people, cosmic powers and spiritual interiorities. Further, if our focus is on ripples of transformation, then our work among the poor is about *movements, not just projects*.

It is time for the Christian response to the poor to mature into initiating movements rather than being content with successful projects. We need to pursue ripples of transformation instead of being content with sporadic transformational events. The challenge is to create a world that does not tolerate poverty—not just transform the poor.

Poverty demands a response that is essentially spiritual at its core

Another theme emerging from this inquiry into poverty is the fact that there are fundamental spiritual issues underlying poverty relationships. The god complexes are molded by spiritual interiorities. Broken relationships and marred identities are essentially a challenge to God's intention for creation. Worldviews, and especially a worldview's religious roots, make our encounter with poverty an encounter not just at the worldview level but an encounter of religious persuasions. Poverty is about truth, and transformation an encounter of truths. Finally, poverty demands an encounter with the principalities and powers.

Therefore, I suggest that poverty by its very nature demands a spiritual response. We need to respond at a level that goes deeper than our traditional level of engagement. We need to expand our scope from addressing dignity issues to clarifying the very identity of the poor. Our community organization has to go beyond mobilizing the poor to creating covenantal communities that are patterned after Yahweh's covenant with his people. We need to move from flesh and blood strategies to including "communicating the mysteries" to the powers in heavenly places. Transformation also includes worldview level engagement with the proclamation of truth.

In many ways this model of transformation demands an engagement or encounter at the level of spiritualities. Transformation is about calling attention to defining the nature of the spiritual—a spirituality that shapes and molds all of life (attitudes, relationships, worldview and behavior). We cannot be agents of transformation without a fundamental undergirding at the spiritual level. There can be no sustainability and empowerment without addressing the spiritual. This is just more than evangelism plus social action. It is an analysis of poverty that recognizes the all-pervading nature of spiritualities and a model of transformation that is essentially spiritual in nature.

Transformation must include transforming the agents of transformation

This issue is closely related to the theme of spirituality. The emerging model of transformation is not only spiritual, but also demands an investment of the person. For example, rebuilding relationships and forming covenantal communities demands investing in relationships. A key question, therefore, is, Have our models of transformation enabled us to invest in relationships? If we will have to challenge a flawed understanding of power then we need to demonstrate what the new understanding is. If we are to clarify identities we need to affirm the image of God in ourselves, as well as in our colleagues. If transformation is about truth then we need to live truth; we should not gloss over lies as the "usual organizational politics."

Years of work among the poor have taught us that limiting our investment among the poor to just money makes the poor beggars, and limiting our investment to programs makes the poor glorified beggars (beneficiaries), but if we believe transformation is about transforming lives then we must intentionally invest our lives. Only life can reproduce life.

If transformation is about investing lives then we must pay attention to the quality of our lives. We must graduate to becoming communities where celebration, diversity and accountability are important hallmarks. If we are called to proclaim truth we must recognize we are fulfilling the prophetic function; we need to become a prophetic community that knows the discipline of standing in "the counsel of the Lord" before rushing to help people. If our transformation is about challenging principalities and powers, then we must be equipped with the whole armor of God, the gifts of the Spirit and prayer and fasting as tools for social action.

If our transformational initiatives must have the mark of integrity, then the agents of transformation must continuously be transformed themselves. We are involved among the poor and the oppressed as obedient followers of the Lord Jesus Christ. Transformation is about obedience and discipleship. Let transformation begin with us.

Notes

[1] "Power deflation," according to Anthony Giddens, is the "spiraling diminution of 'confidence' in the agencies of power so that those subordinate to them come increasingly to question their position" (see Cassell 1993, 223).

[2] Wink's primary thesis in *Engaging the Powers* is that we need to avoid the "cosmic personifications that disguise the power arrangement of the state [and the] . . . mystification of actual power relations that provided divine legitimacy for oppressive earthly institutions" (1992, 25). However, I do not see the need to depersonal-

ize cosmic forces or principalities and powers to understand the relationship between cosmic forces and structures and systems. Wink's description of the domination system appears to be about the power of structures rather than the cosmic powers in structures. I will deal with the role of personal principalities and powers in poverty situations later in this chapter.

³ Marxists, the dependency school and liberation theologians have contributed much to understanding the role of the historical processes in causing poverty.

⁴ First, in poverty studies the focus must be both on macro- as well as micro-realities. However, in the past the focus has been very much on the macro-level historical process, with very little attention given to micro-level historical process. In this chapter I have kept my focus on: (a) the micro-level, thus keeping the focus at the grassroots level; (b) the interpretations of history rather than the objective aspects of history. At the micro-level the focus is not on history as foolproof objective evidence but on particular interpretations of history. Therefore, this study understands history as *interpreted* and looks at its impact on the present and the future; (c) the *remembered* aspects of history that are crucial. The remembered aspects of interpreted history shape the day-to-day lives of the poor. This history is stored in the community's "memory"; and (d) history in the form available as community property. History is a *community process*. The community shares this remembered history.

⁵ Journalist Saritha Rai, narrating the story of a community of prostitutes in the Kolar area (Karnataka, India), points out that the *jathi sampradaya* (the caste tradition) has been used to maintain the institution of prostitution in this village for generations. Caste traditions require that poor families dedicate at least one girl to the trade of prostitution. Fear and shame accompany these traditions. Consequently, traditions and the fear of shame have for generations shaped the identity of this community (see Saritha Rai, "Turning a New Leaf: A Village Steeped in Prostitution Finds a New Life," *India Today* 17, no. 6 [1992], 10).

⁶ Dennis Goulet suggests that these moral options ought to be exercised around three vital issues. They are the criteria of the good life, the basis for just relations in society and the principles for adopting a proper stance toward the forces of nature including technology (Goulet 1989, 45).

⁷ According to the studies of Bruce R. Reichenbach, the theory of karma is embedded in five basic presuppositions:

a. All actions for which we can be held morally accountable and which are done out of a desire for their fruits have [negative] consequences.

b. Moral actions, as actions, have consequences according to the character of the actions performed: right actions have good consequences, wrong actions have bad consequences.

c. Some consequences are manifested immediately or in this life, some in the next life and some remotely.

d. The effects of a karmi's action can be accumulated.

e. Human persons are reborn into the world (Reichenbach 1990, 13–23).

⁸ Heinrich Schlier develops the thesis that the "air" in Ephesians 2:2 is the principal medium by which the powers exercise their control on the affairs of humans (Schlier 1961, 12). H. Berkhof proposed that these powers are structures of earthly existence, and Paul's emphasis is not so much on the personal-spiritual aspects of nature as on the role of the powers in conditioning earthly life (Berkhof 1962, 18). Oscar Cullmann (in *Christ and Time*) proposed that the powers were both human authorities and angelic powers (Arnold 1989, 44). Wesley Carr in a recent work claims that the powers should not be understand as referring to any evil or demonic force but as pure angelic beings who surround the throne of God (Carr 1981). John Howard

Yoder focuses his attention on the "revolutionary subordination" of the church to the "powers." Referring to the identity of the "powers," Yoder points out that they are fallen. However, "the Powers [are] not simply something limitlessly evil. The Powers, despite their fallenness, continue to exercise an ordering function" (Yoder 1972, 143–44). Richard J. Mouw suggests that Paul depersonalizes the power while he identifies these powers as the forces that "'stand behind' and 'influence' the political life [añd] . . . other areas of human social life" (Mouw 1976, 87). Clinton E. Arnold, in his survey of the concept of power in Ephesians, concludes that Paul does not "demythologize the 'powers' and make them equivalent to the abstract notions of 'flesh' and 'sin' or see them as some kind of spiritual 'atmosphere.' The flesh and the devil (with his power) work in confluence leading humanity into disobedience from God" (Arnold 1989, 69). Finally, Walter Wink's three-part work suggests that spiritual powers are not some separate heavenly or ethereal entity but the "inner aspect of material or tangible manifestations of power" (Wink 1984, 104). Wink identifies such an understanding about powers as a mark of an integral worldview based on the views of Carl Jung and others. They are "withinness or interiority in all things, . . . [the] inner spiritual reality [that is] inextricably related to an outer concentration or physical manifestation" (Wink 1992, 5). Wink suggests that there are three types of manifestations of powers. They are the outer personal possession, collective possession and the inner personal demonic (Wink 1986, 43). For Walter Wink, powers are that spiritual interiority of the domination system, which shapes the day-to-day life of all humans.

⁹ Recent interpretations suggest the powers work through economic and political structures, as well as influence social patterns, cultural norms and group habits. "These structures of existence are then viewed as the objects of our spiritual struggle and may be regarded as demonic" (Arnold 1992, 167). On the other hand, there are others who have held the view that powers must only be dealt with in the context of setting individual souls free from the grip of darkness (see survey, McAlpine 1991, 55). C. Peter Wagner points out that the devil and his forces influence nations and keep the minds of the unreached blind. Wagner argues, based on his reflections on passages like Daniel 10:10–21, that the "territorial spirits and their dominance of geographical areas are taken for granted as the history of Israel unfolds" (Wagner and Pennmoyer 1990, 79). However, Walter Wink, as mentioned earlier, is of the opinion that the powers are the inner spirituality that inhabits structures and systems. He suggests that unless we depersonalize the cosmic powers, it will be difficult to justify any involvement in setting right the inadequacies in structures and systems (Wink 1992). Clinton E. Arnold, commenting on the influence of the powers over nations and territories, suggests that the powers influence structures and systems by influencing people (Arnold 1992, 202). Thus the influence of the powers "extends to human institutions and organizations, the social and political order" (Arnold 1992, 81). There is much ambiguity about the role of the powers in relation to structures and systems. Richard Mouw points out that this ambiguity is not due to defects in current theological understanding, but due to "the perils inherent in attempts to duplicate Paul's exact views, given his lack of systematic presentation on the subject" (1976, 88). Since the focus of this paper is on the role of the personal principalities and powers, I would like to consider their role as such without reducing them to structures of existence or interiorities. These personal cosmic powers do influence structures.

¹⁰ I use the term *lie* to qualify particular assumptions within the worldview of persons within poverty relationships. My understanding of poverty situations, in the light of scriptural affirmations about humans being made in the image of God and

other such foundational truths, suggests that the term *lie* aptly describes the contrary assumptions that create and sustain poverty and powerlessness. However, there is need for further comparative inquiry between biblical affirmations and worldview assumptions within poverty relationships.

References and Recommended Reading

Appasamy, A. J. 1942. *The Gospel and India's Heritage*. New York: Macmillan.

Arnold, Clinton E. 1989. *Ephesians—Power and Magic: The Concept of Power in Ephesians in the Light of Its Historical Setting*. Grand Rapids, Mich.: Baker House.

———. 1992. *Powers of Darkness: Principalities and Powers in Paul's Letters*. Downers Grove, Ill.: Inter Varsity Press.

Berkhof, H. 1962. *Christ and the Powers*. Scottdale, Pa.: Herald Press.

Brueggemann, Walter. 1978. *The Prophetic Imagination*. Philadelphia: Fortress Press.

Carr, Wesley. 1981. *Angels and Principalities: The Background, Meaning and Development of the Pauline Phrase hai archai kai hai exousiai* SNTSMS 42: Cambridge University Press.

Cassell, Philip. 1993. *The Giddens*. Stanford, Calif.: Stanford University Press.

Chambers, Robert. 1983. *Rural Development: Putting the Last First*. Essex, UK: Longman Scientific and Technical.

———. 1988. *Poverty in India: Concepts, Research and Reality*. Sussex, UK: Institute of Development Studies.

———. 1991. "In Search of Professionalism, Bureaucracy and Sustainable Livelihoods for the 21st Century." *IDS Bulletin* 22, no. 4: 5–11.

Christian, Jayakumar. 1994. "Powerlessness of the Poor: Toward an Alternative Kingdom of God Based Paradigm for Response." Pasadena, Calif.: Fuller Theological Seminary.

Cullmann, Oscar. 1964. *Christ and Time*. Philadelphia: Westminster Press.

Curtis, Michael, ed. 1981. *The Great Political Theories*. Vol. 2. New York: Avon Books.

Doyal, Len, and Ian Gough. 1991. *Theory of Human Need*. New York: The Guilford Press.

Duncan, Michael. 1990. *A Journey in Development: The Bridge Series*. Melbourne, Australia: World Vision.

Friedmann, John. 1992. *Empowerment: The Politics of Alternative Development*. Cambridge, Mass.: Blackwell.

Freire, Paulo. 1990. *Pedagogy of the Oppressed*. New York: Continuum.

———. 1993. *Pedagogy of the City*. New York: Continuum.

Goulet, Dennis. 1989. *The Uncertain Promise: Value Conflicts in Technology Transfer.* New York: New Horizons Press.

Hiebert, Paul. 1982. "The Flaw of the Excluded Middle," *Missiology* 10, no. 1.

Kearney, Michael. 1984. *Worldview*. Novato, Calif.: Chandler and Sharp.

Kraft, Charles H. 1989. *Christianity with Power: Your Worldview and Your Experience of the Supernatural*. Ann Arbor, Mich.: Servant Publications.

———. 1990. "Response to 'In Dark Dungeons of Collective Captivity' by Pennoyer." In Wagner and Pennoyer, *Wrestling with Dark Angels*.

———. 1992. *Defeating the Dark Angels: Breaking Demonic Oppression in the Believer's Life*. Ann Arbor, Mich.: Servant Publications.

Kuppuswamy, B. 1992. *Social Change in India*. 4th edition. Delhi: Konark Publishers.

Liddle, R. William. 1992. "The Politics of Development Policy." *World Development* 20, no. 6.

Linthicum, Robert C. 1991. *Empowering the Poor: Community Organizing Among the City's "Rag, Tag and Bobtail."* Monrovia, Calif.: MARC.

Llosa, Mario Vargas. 1989. "Foreword." In *The Other Path: The Invisible Revolution in the Third World,* edited by Hernando De Soto. New York: Harper & Row.

McAlpine, Thomas H. 1991. *Facing the Powers: What Are the Options?* Monrovia, Calif.: MARC.

Mahadevan, T.M.P. 1956. *Outlines of Hinduism.* Bombay: Chetna.

Mills, C. Wright. 1993. "The Structure of Power in American Society." In *Power in Modern Societies,* edited by Marvin E. Olsen and Martin N. Marger. Boulder, Colo.: Westview Press.

Mouw, Richard J. 1976. *Politics and the Biblical Drama.* Grand Rapids, Mich.: Wm. B. Eerdmans.

Mills, Wright C. 1959. *The Power Elite.* New York: Oxford University Press.

Myers, Bryant. 1991. "The Excluded Middle," *MARC Newsletter* 91, no. 2: 3.

Newbigin, Lesslie. 1966. *Honest Religion for Secular Man.* Philadelphia: Westminster Press.

Ng, Sik Hung. 1980. *The Social Psychology of Power.* London: Academic Press.

Olsen, Marvin E., and Martin N. Marger. 1990. "In Dark Dungeons of Collective Captivity." In *Wrestling with Dark Angels: Toward a Deeper Understanding of the Supernatural Forces in Spiritual Warfare,* edited by C. Peter Wagner and F. Douglas Pennoyer. Ventura, Calif.: Regal Books.

Olsen, Marvin E., and Martin N. Marger, eds. 1993. *Power in Modern Societies.* Boulder, Colo.: Westview Press.

Prabhu, Pandharinath. 1940. *Hindu Social Organization: A Study in Socio-Psychological and Ideological Foundations.* Bombay, India: Popular Prakashan.

Radhakrishnan, Sarvapalli. 1927. *The Hindu View of Life.* Bombay, India: Blackie & Sons Publishers.

Rao, Nagaraja P. 1983. "Hinduism and the Common Man." In *The Gospel Among Our Hindu Neighbours,* edited by Vinay Samuel and Chris Sugden. Bangalore, India: Asian Trading Corporation.

Rappaport, Julian. 1987. "Terms of Empowerment/Exemplars of Prevention: Toward a Theory for Community Psychology." *American Journal of Community Psychology* 15, no. 2:121–48.

Reichenbach, Bruce R. 1990. *The Law of Karma: A Philosophical Study.* Honolulu: University of Hawaii Press.

Schlier, Heinrich. 1961. *Principalities and Powers in the New Testament.* London: Nelson.

Wagner, C. Peter, and F. Douglas Pennoyer, eds. 1990. *Wrestling with Dark Angels: Toward a Deeper Understanding of the Supernatural Forces in Spiritual Warfare,* Ventura, Calif.: Regal Books.

Wink, Walter. 1984. *Naming the Powers: The Language of Power in the New Testament.* Philadelphia.: Fortress Press.

———. 1986. *Unmasking the Powers: The Invisible Forces that Determine Human Existence.* Philadelphia: Fortress Press.

———. 1992. *Engaging the Powers: Discernment and Resistance in a World of Domination.* Philadelphia: Fortress Press.

Wrong, Dennis H. 1979. *Power: Its Forms, Bases and Uses.* New York: Harper & Row.

Yoder, John Howard. 1972. *The Politics of Jesus.* Grand Rapids, Mich.: Wm. B. Eerdmans.

PART TWO

METHODS

2

Holistic Participatory Learning and Action

Seeing the Spiritual and Whose Reality Counts

RAVI I. JAYAKARAN

CONTROLLING INFLUENCES IN A COMMUNITY

In the introduction to *Worshipping False Gods*, Arun Shourie writes: "A nation forges deities in its imaginings, in its sacred literature, in wood and stone. The forms it gives them, the forces it has them embody, the virtues with which it endows them reflect the accumulated experience of the nation, the insights of its seers, the answer to its needs." It is obvious that the gods a community worships and its beliefs about the spiritual realm reflect how that community views reality. How sad it is to discover that Christian development workers have chosen to ignore this very area while striving to understand the communities with which we work.

In recent years major paradigm shifts have been made in community development work. There has been increasing recognition that "top down" externally conceived solutions do not solve the problems of communities, nor are such solutions sustainable. It is important to understand a community's view of reality. This realization has now moved beyond the realms of nongovernmental organizations to influence major development agencies, universities and government agencies, all of which have now started using Participatory Learning and Action (PLA) on a wider scale. Christian development agencies, however, have fallen short of learning from others the crucial need to understand the spiritual reality of communities as the community sees it.

Holistic PLAs can aid us to understand more fully and to analyze the holistic worldview of the communities with which we work. This analysis recognizes each dimension that influences a community's survival strategies and helps us understand the specific influence these dimensions have on the

31

community's life. For example, research has shown that communities in the Nagpur area see three main controlling influences in their lives:

1. areas influenced by god(s);
2. areas influenced by outsiders;
3. areas over which the community itself has influence.

These three controlling influences play a role in each aspect of the community's survival strategy. For instance, a particular village may depend on the following for survival:

- agriculture
- animal husbandry
- herbal medication
- minor forest produce collection
- electricity
- local market
- communication (roads)

The community believes that the three major influences have an impact of one kind or another on these aspects for survival. The impact of each of these influences will vary from community to community. For example, various influences on agriculture for three different villages may be as follows:

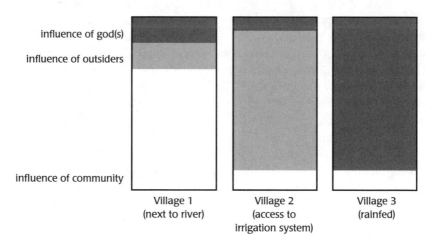

Figure 2–1: Comparison of three villages.

The areas of greatest uncertainty are assigned to a god. A visit to each village will show the position the community gives to the god of rainfall. In village 3 the god of rainfall will be perceived as the most important influence, since the whole village depends on rainfed agriculture. Villages 1 and 2 have access to a dependable water source but also have a marginal dependence on the deity controlling rainfall, because rain can come down at the wrong time and damage a crop.

A COMMUNITY'S WORLDVIEW

As one looks at each aspect of a survival strategy the areas of influence would vary from village to village. Ethnographic studies of these villages may reveal the same people group or religious background, but an analysis of their holistic worldview may show a totally different profile than one would originally assume exists. The Ten Seed Technique, developed by the author and mentioned below, can reveal the proportion of control a community ascribes to each major influencer—a god, outsiders and the community.

This technique is especially useful in ascertaining a community's worldview on the basis of the community's capability and vulnerability profile rather than its stated religious belief. For instance, in Dighori village in the Nagpur region, we assumed the community, since it was predominantly Neo-Buddhist, would have a Buddhist worldview. To the contrary, we found that the gods and spirits that influenced the lives of community members were the ones that controlled the community's areas of vulnerability—the gods that controlled rainfall, disease and wild animals. Buddha, the god they professed belief in, only influenced their "peace of mind." The overriding influences in their lives remain largely determined by the way they see reality. Thus even communities that claim to be Christian, but have not had their worldviews transformed, are likely to forge deities to address their vulnerabilities or try to twist God to fulfill a utilitarian role. Some discipling processes only change behavior; others change behavior and beliefs, but leave the worldview unaltered. By default, the worldview becomes the overriding dominating influence. The first step in making holistic disciples is to understand a person's (or community's) worldview, and then begin the process of discipling.

THE PROCESS OF DISCIPLING

We can imagine the process of discipling as three concentric circles. The largest is *behavior* change, the area most prone to change by external influence. Within this circle is the deeper area of *beliefs*, which needs stronger penetrative indoctrination to bring about change. The controlling center is the *worldview* (or being), and if it is not properly understood, analyzed and "discipled," it will by default revert to its original worldview. Thus when the external influences of change are withdrawn, the "undiscipled" worldview will take over.

A survival strategy consists of various activities a community undertakes to hold its world together. When we examine these activities, we see them as capabilities and vulnerabilities in a community's survival strategy. Aspects under the community's direct control are seen as capabilities, and those under indirect control are seen as vulnerabilities. This is the development agency's view of reality, however; to the community there is a seamless continuum between the directly controlled and indirectly controlled—between the empirical and the supernatural. Thus, whenever a development agency identifies what it considers an area of vulnerability, in the eyes of the community it is an area well within its control, albeit indirect control. The development agency's intentions to intervene are thus seen as conflicting with the existing supernatural order.

A community's survival strategy may show the marginalization of a god, when the community turns to the god only when dealing with an area of uncertainty. As the community's circle of control widens with access to resources and skills, the god may be pushed out of that particular aspect. Perhaps this gives us greater insight into what has happened to affluent Western communities, which have developed survival strategies that, by bringing more uncertainties under their immediate control, have pushed God out of playing an active role in their lives.

COMMUNITY UNDERSTANDING

Holistic PLA also enables us to perceive how the community understands messages we are attempting to communicate. In Gohekhurd village we discovered that the community had a different understanding from our staff of how one approaches God. The community believed that the more powerful the god, the less frequently that god was to be approached, and then never by individuals—it was always to be a whole village together or several villages together. Our staff, on the other hand, spoke about a God who interacts with individuals on a personal level and who actually comes to the door and knocks. This idea didn't make sense to the community, because it made them believe our God was not very powerful and therefore unworthy of their attention.

To the communities with whom we work, we ourselves do not come across as a community, with a community's vibrant and supportive relational interaction. They see us as a group of individuals who are hierarchically aligned. Community members deal with staff as different individuals with whom they meet, rather than as people who are part of a community. Therefore the profile of the individual they interact with plays a major role. Individuals can interact only with the particular caste group they belong to. This attitude is especially strong in the rural areas of Maharashtra and Karnataka, where caste plays a dominant role. Since a person's name communicates the caste he or she belongs to, an Anglicized or "Christian" name is assumed to be a "cover up" for someone from a lower caste.

The strong caste system is a major barrier to our work. Except in the tribal areas of the states of Maharashtra, Gujarat and Karnataka, major parts of rural areas in these states are very strongly influenced by caste. In the Vidharba region of Maharashtra, there are villages where some of our staff have no influence because of their origins and family background. Having to operate within this framework restricts the efficiency of the transformational development process, but it is a reality we must acknowledge.

At the base of ethnocentricity is *attitude* (see the figure below). The community's attitude to a particular thing results in *prejudice*. A strong attitude may have a *history* behind it and thus result in a strong prejudice for or against a particular stand. In due course this attitude becomes manifest in a form of ethnocentricity, shaping cultural practices that lend the community justifiable reasons for its particular stand.

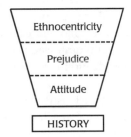

Figure 2–2: The ethnocentricity framework.

Change must therefore take place at the level of attitude before we can overcome prejudice or change ethnocentricity. A community's experiential history plays a vital role in shaping its attitude. Hence it is important to listen to and explore the community's history as community members perceive it if we want to even begin to understand what their attitude is.

SUMMARY

1. Understanding the community's reality "as the people see it" is mandatory for effective Christian witness. The community's reality counts.

2. Our experience in using holistic PLA has shown that when we listen to a community and try to understand its reality, we find its worldview is very different from what we expected it to be. Often, because of each community's experiential history, those with similar ethnographic profiles have divergent worldviews.

3. Communities must be empowered to share their worldviews, to tell their stories. This involves using active processes such as holistic PLA.

4. Communities have definite understandings about the causes and effects related to their circumstances and the issues facing them. Development workers must let communities present their understanding of the causes and effects of matters that have an impact on communities' survival strategies.

5. Finally, our effectiveness in understanding a community's reality depends on how well we can make a paradigm shift in our approach.

A FINAL NOTE ON USING HOLISTIC PLA

PLA has been used successfully in development circles for several years. The method is starting to gain ground with larger development agencies and government departments. It has found wide-scale application for generating new insights into subjects such as demographic profiles, education, health, agriculture, afforestation, rural and urban integrated community development, relief and development, children's programs, marriage counseling and AIDS awareness. More recently PLA methodology has been modified and expanded to go beyond the empirical to facilitate a better understanding of the supernatural dimension, to include its use in carrying out a holistic worldview analysis, and for measuring issues of Christian witness.

Organizations can put holistic PLAs to widespread use in area development programs. During the part of the method's exercise where the worldview analysis diagram is made and completed, there is scope for us to discuss with the community what its assessment of the "perfect god" is—someone who could deal with every aspect of their lives, helping them to become better stewards of their capabilities and enabling them to deal with their vulnerabilities effectively.

This would essentially work toward bringing God actively into the area of their capabilities—that part of their survival strategy within their control—and also bring about an integration of the several smaller "God needs." This would be the first step in discipling their worldview. The second step would be to bring about further integration to show that the same God can deal with both their vulnerabilities and capabilities.

In the development world there is still much resistance to doing anything differently from current practice. Work like this, because it challenges earlier presuppositions, can be very threatening. However, if we believe what Jesus said about being willing to be like a seed that falls and dies before it brings forth a stem, leaves and finally fruit, then I believe we are at the threshold of a new beginning.

For further reading

Arulappa, R.. *Thirukkural and Its Central Thought*. Meipporul Publishers, 1990.
Basham, A. L. *The Wonder that Was India*. Rupa and Co., 1996.
Chambers, Robert. *Whose Reality Counts?* Intermediate Technology Publication, 1997.
Chaudhuri, Nirad C. *Hinduism: A Religion to Live By*. Oxford India Paperbacks, 1996.
———. *The Continent of Circle*. Jaico Publishing House, 1997.
Colson, Charles. *Kingdoms in Conflict*. Hodder and Stoughton, 1984.

David, George. *Communicating Christ Among Hindu People*. CBMTM, 1998.

Deivanayagam, M., and D. Devakala. *Christianity in Hinduism*. Dravidian Religious Trust, Aug. 97.

Dharma Deepika. Madras, India: Deepika Educational Trust, 1997.

Drucker, Peter F. "The New Realities." *Harper Business*, 1989.

Government of India Planning Commission. *Training Calendar*. Planning Commission 1998.

Hedlund, Roger E. *God and the Nations*. ISPCK, Delhi 1997.

Hiebert, Paul G. *Anthropological Reflections on Missiological Issues*. Baker Books 1994.

Hinduism: The Eternal Religion. Visnosoft—CD-ROM.

Karishma. Interactive CD-ROM on India.

Mair, Jessie H. *Bungalows in Heaven*. GLS, 1993.

Mangalwadi, Vishal. *Letters to a Postmodern Hindu*. Nivedit Good Books, 1996.

Murichan, J., S.J. *Poverty in India*. A Xavier Board Publication, 1988.

Pye-Smith, Charles. *Rebels and Outcasts*. Viking, Penguin Group, 1997.

Radhakrishnan, S. *Faith Renewed*. Hind Pocket Books, 1995.

———. *The Spirit of Religion*. Hind Pocket Books, 1995.

Sangharakshita. *Ambedkar and Buddhism*. Windhorse, 1986.

———. *A Survey of Buddhism*. Trinatna Granthmala, 1996.

Kim, Sebastian C. H., and Krickwin C. Marak. *Good News to the Poor*. CMS/ISPCK, 1997.

Shourie, Arun. *Worshipping False Gods*. Harper Collins, 1997.

Uplekar, Mukund, and Sheela Rangan. *Tackling TB*. FRCH, 1996.

Yisudas, G. D. *Are All Religions the Same?* GLS, Nov. 1994.

3

Capacity Building Using
the Appreciative Inquiry Approach

DIRK BOOY AND SARONE OLE SENA

HISTORICAL APPROACHES TO CAPACITY BUILDING

Throughout the modern history of education and development, interventions have matured from emptiness based (banking approach) to weakness based (problem solving) and finally to strength based (Appreciative Inquiry). All three approaches remain in use in community development. The first approach assumes that rural and urban communities are "empty," lacking capacities, skills, hope, spirit and resources to build upon. The second approach assumes that communities are "half empty" or weak, with many problems. Through community participation the situation can be improved, provided that bottlenecks and problems are fixed. The third approach builds on existing community capacities and strengths assumed to be present in every rural and urban setting. Appreciative Inquiry assumes the principle of "the glass is half full, not half empty," and it is strength based.

Each of these approaches continues to contribute to development theory and practice. Our premise is that the appreciative mode is inherently powerful and filled with potential, and is infinitely more generative than the other modes. Appreciative Inquiry recognizes the miracle and mystery of commUNITY and invites community members to discover, learn about and nurture life-giving resources and skills that foster innovation and the creation of new possibilities. Let's take a closer look at each approach.

The banking approach

For years traditional education has been seen as a process of passing on valuable information and knowledge from one person who knows (the teacher) to others who do not know (the students). Paulo Freire[1] refers to this process as "banking education"—the teacher makes regular deposits in the empty mind of the student. It has also been described as pouring water from a jug into an empty glass, or compared to filling an empty car tank with fuel.

In the development field this banking approach dominated before the 1980s and still continues to some extent. James Mayfield[2] argues that in the 1950s development was done *to* the people. Capital and technical transfer and investment were priorities, and communities were seen as separate from the development process. In the 1960s development was done *for* the people. Communities were recipients of development but not active players. In the 1970s development was done *through* the people. Communities provided the process for achieving development, but activity was still orchestrated from outside the community. The banking approach presumes that development not only adds something new but comes from outside the community in question.[3] This approach disregards the experience communities have before the arrival of development planners.

Proponents of the banking approach generally support blueprint strategies to community capacity building. Communities are ignored as potential resources. Hans Deiter Seibel and Andreas Massing, David Korten, Michael M. Cernea, and Bernard J. Lecomte state that communities are seen by some international donor agencies, development planners, governments and NGOs as a hindrance to development.[4] Community culture and institutions are perceived as constraints on modernization, remnants of old times and nuisances to be eliminated in order to "really modernize." In short, communities with their local institutions are said to be "empty," and their role, involvement and participation in capacity-building interventions are ignored.

The problem-solving approach

Educational thinking shifted from teacher-based learning prior to the 1980s to participatory learning, in which students were provided frameworks for thinking, describing, analyzing, suggesting, considering problems and finding possible solutions.

Development, meanwhile, began being done *with* the people. Local participation by communities became a necessary ingredient in development. Communities were considered as catalysts or partners in development. Villagers became actively involved in the social construction of knowledge. Development planners sought community cooperation in the problem-solving process. From the beginning, participants in a project or program were recognized as thinking, reflective people with some capacity for action. The aim of a development facilitator became to help community members identify aspects of their lives they wished to change: to identify problems, find root causes of these problems, and work out practical ways in which community members could set about changing the situation.

This mode is often described as a participatory search for solutions to problems. In the words of Paulo Freire:

> Problem-posing education is prophetic, and as such is hopeful, corresponding to the historical nature of human beings. It affirms people as beings who transcend themselves, who move forward and look ahead, for whom looking at the past must only be a means of understanding more clearly what and who they are, so that they can more wisely build the future.[5]

The problem-solving approach argues that no one has all the answers and that no one is totally ignorant. Each person has different perceptions based on his or her own experience. To discover valid solutions to problems, everyone needs to be both a learner and a teacher. Education and development become mutual learning processes. The role of the development facilitator is to create a situation in which genuine dialogue can take place in the community, where each shares experience, listens to and learns from the others.

Korten[6] and others have documented the advantages of this learner-based methodology that is problem-focused. The problem-solving approach is credited with developing community capacity to (a) embrace error, (b) plan with development partners, and (c) link knowledge-building with action. Advocates also assert that this approach promotes community empowerment.

Appreciative Inquiry

Problem solving encourages rural and urban communities to celebrate successes constantly as well as analyze critically the causes of mistakes and failures in order to find solutions to problems. The appreciative approach agrees with the celebrating of past successes and builds upon the best of the past, as well as peak experiences and successes of the present.

Appreciative Inquiry (AI) processes build the capacity of communities on the foundation of what works; what empowers; what gives energy, joy, happiness, motivation, hope and inspiration. AI builds upon small accomplishments by communities and, rather than going back to mistakes and failures made, instead encourages communities to reflect on conditions that produced successes. Individuals are given opportunity to articulate their community's best features based on their own experiences:

- What do I value most about my community?
- When in my community's history did we experience a high point?
- What do I want my community to pass on to future generations?
- What image of my community do we want to promote?

- What traditions do we value most?
- What has worked well for me and my community and why?

If people can see where they have succeeded in the past and understand why, and if they can build on this to plan for a better future, they may be able to attain greater success. The emphasis on looking for successes (best practices) stems partly from a principle called the *heliotropic effect*. In biology this refers to plants' natural tendency to turn toward the light. In social systems the heliotropic effect refers to the natural affinity communities have toward those things that give them energy and joy. Movement toward those things is more natural and easier than moving away from problems or difficulties (see Figure 3–1).

Factor	Banking approach	Problem-solving approach	Appreciative Inquiry approach
Assumption	Emptiness based	Weakness based	Strength based
Communities	Ignore	Cooperate	Co-create
Focus	What doesn't exist?	What is wrong?	What is best?
Principle	Clean slate	Communities as machines	Heliotropic effect
Approach	"Stuck" or passive	Adaptive or reative	Generative or creative
Capacity building	Do to communities	Do with communities	Affirm/empower communities

Figure 3–1: Comparison of three approaches.

One of the great differences among the three methods is the approach taken toward analysis.[7] AI, through its use of the narrative and storytelling process, takes a whole-systems approach. Nothing is broken down into component parts. Instead, people draw from their whole experience, and only after having told their stories (and thus relived their experiences) do they pay attention to themes that surface. Through storytelling people bring their whole selves to the act of co-creating. The problem-solving method is inherently reactive (adaptive), taking all cues from the current situation. Appreciative Inquiry is inherently creative (generative), and the result cannot be guessed ahead of time.

A community effort to change built on an appreciative approach can be viewed as a journey, but not the kind planned well in advance with "hotel rooms reserved" at each stop.[8] This journey involves more adventure and risk, because a process guides the general direction but allows for unexpected side trips. Throughout the journey, hope based on past accomplishments grows—hope that things can be better, that individual and community dreams can be achieved.

USING APPRECIATIVE INQUIRY
TO BUILD CAPACITY

Appreciative Inquiry affirms existing capacity

Around the world nongovernmental organizations (NGOs), community-based organizations, international agencies, governments, universities and donors are discovering an inescapable lesson: the fight against poverty and environmental decline requires new approaches, new opportunities, new initiatives and an alternative community development path. The focus of the 1990s for most development agencies has been on developing local capacity for self-development.[9] Caroline Sahley captures it in these words:

> Building local capacity for social and economic development, rather than merely transferring resources, or filling technological and financial gaps, is now recognized as the key to sustainable development.[10]

Appreciative Inquiry was developed in the mid-1970s by David Cooperrider and his colleagues in the Department of Organizational Behavior at the Weatherhead School of Management, Case Western Reserve University, Cleveland, Ohio, USA. Drawing on research and writings from diverse fields such as organizational behavior, sociology, psychology, education, anthropology, sports, and on his own extensive experience in working with organizations, Cooperrider developed an evolving set of AI concepts and theories now being put into practice and shaped by the contributions of field practitioners worldwide.

Among the most important concepts underlying Appreciative Inquiry is that *image and action are linked*—successful organizations and communities have a positive guiding image widely shared that galvanizes action. Also, organizations and communities *move in the direction of the questions they ask*—the kinds of questions asked in organizations and communities determine what the organizations and communities find, and what is found sets the direction of the journey. All organizations and communities *have something about their past and present to value*—the stronger the focus on what worked in the past, and what is going well today, the more vibrant the dream of the future. Organizations and communities *are not fixed*—virtually any pattern, system, structure, belief, attitude or habit created by humans is open to alteration. And finally, *building appreciative skills* is a key leadership task—appreciative leaders are those who notice and heighten positive potential in an individual, organization or community and see radical possibilities beyond the boundaries of problems and weaknesses.[11]

Miracle and mystery

Appreciative Inquiry finds its starting point in one of the most ancient archetypes of hope and inspiration known to humankind—the miracle and mystery of life. In the same way that the birth of a living, breathing, thinking and feeling human being is a mystery, the birth and development of living, breathing, thinking and feeling human systems can be considered a miracle of cooperative human behavior for which there can never be a final explanation.

So, at its core, Appreciative Inquiry takes a philosophical stance that recognizes the miracle and mystery of collective life and invites us to explore it, with the wonder and awe of a small child, in order to discover new and better ways of living and working together. AI gets us out of the mode of constant focusing on problems and into a mode of continuous innovation.[12]

How does Appreciative Inquiry work?

Development practitioners often ask, "On a more practical level, how does AI work? How does one do an Appreciative Inquiry?" Appreciative Inquiry is a capacity-building process that begins by (1) valuing the organization or community, and the culture in which it is embedded; (2) learning about the organization or community, its relationships and its environment; and (3) discovering and building upon existing strengths. AI seeks out the very best of "what is" to help ignite the collective imagination of "what might be." The aim is to generate new knowledge that expands the "realm of the possible" and helps members of an organization or community to envision a collectively desired future and to carry that vision successfully into reality.

A common framework for using Appreciative Inquiry to build community or organizational capacity is the 4–D model (see Figure 3–2). Let's take an appreciative look at each stage of the 4–D model: discovery, dream, design and delivery.

Stage 1: Discovery

The first step is to discover and value factors that give life to a community, an organization, to find the "best of what is." Regardless of how few moments of excellence participants can name, the challenge is to focus in on these and to discuss factors and forces that made excellence possible. Four key questions are asked:

1. Describe a peak experience or high point.
2. What things do you value most about yourself, the nature of your work, the organization or community?

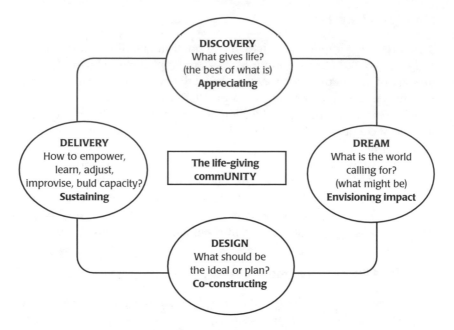

Figure 3–2: The 4–D model.

3. What do you consider to be the core factor that gives life to this organization or community?
4. What three wishes would you make to heighten vitality and health in this organization or community?

Appreciative Inquiry can be an appropriate process at many stages in the life of an organization, a community or a staff team. One group found that the AI discovery phase, after a time of crisis, provided a forum both for talking together about the crisis and for exploring experiences during the crisis, allowing the team to discover strengths on which it could begin to rebuild relationships and new hope.

Stage 2: Dream

This second stage uses discovered knowledge from the first stage to develop an image of how a community or organization might look at some future point. With the best of the past and present actively in mind, members create a model for the future community or organization and its impact in the world that stretches the realm of the status quo, challenges common assumptions or routines and suggests real possibilities. The key here is passionate thinking, allowing members of a community or organization to be inspired by what they have learned in the discovery stage.

Stage 3: Design

After discovery and dreaming comes design. During this stage, community or organizational elements (structure, systems, partnerships, donor relations and learning processes) are considered. Finally, members develop strategic plans to bring about and sustain initiatives for change.

Stage 4: Delivery

As members of the community or organization engage in valuing, envisioning and future building, they grow committed, with a clear sense of where they are headed. Participants find innovative ways to help move the community or organization closer to shared ideals. They take responsibility for innovation and action. Challenges of sustaining momentum, bringing other stakeholders into the process and taking action on provocative propositions are addressed.

But Appreciative Inquiry does not end with delivery. Constructing the future is a beginning, not the end, of sustainable development. If we accept the proposition that commUNITY life is a mystery and miracle, then this final stage must be seen as an opportunity to act on things that have been envisioned and designed and, further, as an ongoing opportunity to set out and discover, understand and nurture continuous learning.

AI and biblical context

The Bible is essentially a message of hope pointing to God's faithfulness and love. Whereas we see a broken world, full of sinfulness and hopelessness, God sees a new creation where all things will be restored to be a delight and a joy (Isa. 65, Rev. 21). The Bible tells us God's plan of redemption and restoration.

We read in Genesis that when God created the world it was *good*. Everything was perfect. Creation was established to honor the Creator. After the Fall, God laid out a redemptive plan that points to the new creation—in which everything will be good again. The focus of the entire biblical narrative is not on humanity's sinfulness or unfaithfulness but on God's faithfulness and restoration of a good creation. God sees beyond our sinfulness and points us to redemption. God sees what can be (the possible) and has a clear plan to bring it about.

Appreciative Inquiry is consistent with the overall biblical message of hope and restoration. AI helps us to focus on God's rich plan of redemption and to be involved in co-creating the new creation. AI can help point us toward the kingdom of God, calling us to live out the hope we find in Christ. Using the 4–D model, Christians can challenge themselves with the following:

Discovery: What gives life to us as children of God? What do we appreciate most about our relationship to God? What three wishes would we make
to heighten our role as kingdom builders?

Dream: What is the Bible calling for? What image is God creating for us
in the new heavens and the new earth? What is our role?

Design: How is God calling us to co-create and bring hope? What can we
do, and how should we be involved? What can we contribute?

Delivery: As the commUNITY of believers, are we part of the exciting
growth and realization of God's kingdom? Are we delivering God's message of hope and restoration?

A CAPACITY-BUILDING MODEL

- When an artist begins to paint a picture, she already has the image in
  her head.
- The strength of a jazz band is its ability to innovate within a mutually
  understood pattern.
- The beauty of childhood is learning to explore the world within the
  safety of a family.

All these images are about celebrating the possible—about reaching beyond the realm of what is to what can be. In the same way, *capacity building
is the art of celebrating the full potential of community or organizational expression, and making that potential a reality.*

Our experience in capacity building can be shown on two broad
continuums: focus and approach. The extremes of the focus continuum are
internal and external. An *external* focus seeks to develop capacity in others.
Partnerships are often defined in stages from dependency to independence
(or interdependency). Consultancy, training, evaluations, staff secondments
may be utilized. An *internal* capacity-building focus seeks to develop capacity within the organization itself, utilizing staff development, organizational
development, management/leadership development and so on.

The end points of the approach continuum are technical and Appreciative Inquiry. A technical approach looks at skills, knowledge, systems and
procedures, and provides technical solutions based on consultancies, training and reports. Emphasis is often on problem resolution and a "fix-it"
approach. Appreciative Inquiry, at the other extreme, seeks to explore opportunities and possibilities as a capacity-building strategy. AI builds on the
best of what is in order to construct the best of what can be. As explained in
the previous section, it is participatory and builds on strengths that already
exist in the community or organization.

As with most descriptions based on continuums, the majority of capacity-building programs find themselves somewhere between the two extremes.

What is important is building synergy between the different approaches and focuses. The two continuums can be joined, as in Figure 3–3, to show how synergy can take place.[13]

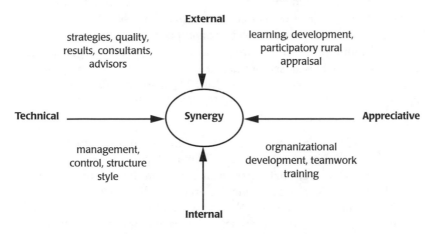

Figure 3–3: A combination framework for capacity building.

There are four quadrants in the diagram. Each represents a combination of both the approach and the focus of the capacity-building intervention. Experience has taught us that effective capacity building requires a holistic integration involving all four quadrants.

A development organization's effectiveness in building the capacity of communities depends on its ability to develop its own internal capacity. In the same way, for the same organization to develop internal capacity, it must interact with external groups in synergistic capacity-building relationships. For a technical capacity-building intervention to be successful, an appreciative format is strategic. The reverse is also true; that is, for Appreciative Inquiry to be successful as a capacity-building activity, it must be balanced by technical interventions.

Sometimes capacity building will start within one of the four quadrants, but its overall success will be determined by the ability to move toward the center of synergy.

Conceptually, an organization's capacity begins with its mission or purpose. This should attract committed and qualified staff and board members, who together build a strong organization. The community can then be empowered by a dynamic and vibrant organization. At the same time, the community's (external) capacity begins building organizational capacity through reciprocal partnerships that enhance the staff and board, which in turn strengthen the mission. Within each capacity-building component specific indicators measure capacity over time. These indicators help to identify, plan and implement interventions.

As synergy increases, the center capacity of holism—the area where community, organization and staff overlap—expands. When highly competent and committed staff work in an efficient and appreciative organization, communities are empowered and enriched. When strong communities achieving their dreams interact with effective organizations, staff are empowered. And when dynamic organizations create appreciative environments for staff capacity, community outcomes are achieved. The dynamic, holistic capacity that results enables all sectors to shine.

In a recent study involving more than 100 partner NGOs, the Christian Reformed World Relief Committee (CRWRC) identified the following critical principles of capacity building:

1. Begin with partnership. Capacity building requires mutually beneficial partnerships that build capacity in both partner entities.
2. Practice appreciation. Create an environment that celebrates the possibilities of capacities and enables dreams to be realized.
3. Contextualize everything. Not every situation is the same. Capacity building needs to be contextualized in each new environment.
4. Think organically. Because organizations are organic systems, capacity-building interventions are enhanced when organic references are used.
5. Emphasize learning. The capacity to learn from success and from error greatly increases organizational development.
6. Create systems of mutual accountability. All partnerships need to be built on mutual trust and accountability that is focused on achieving results.[14]

COMMUNITY CAPACITY BUILDING

Since 1995 we've experimented with using Appreciative Inquiry to build organizational capacity, help form partnerships between organizations, bring multiple organizations together to find common ground, strengthen staff capacity and morale, and empower and finally build community capacity.

Challenges face our staff in many communities attempting to implement AI. Because development paradigms remain steeped in problem solving, communities find it difficult at first to identify their strengths and capacities, insisting that they are needy or even exaggerating their problems in order to receive funding.

In one new area development program in western Tanzania, we began the Appreciative Inquiry process with discovery, asking such questions as these:

- As a people of Kagera Region, what are you most proud of?
- What stories concern your most valued traditions?
- What are your best practices in farming?

- Why have you been so successful in formal education and schooling?
- What core factors make life in Kagera possible?

At first the villagers stared at us, wondering what we were trying to accomplish. Then one teacher stood to say that the villagers have many problems. Children were dying of measles, youth were dying of AIDS, mothers did not have access to prenatal services, fathers did not have enough money to pay school fees for their children, and grandparents were left to care for orphans whose parents had died of AIDS. Other villagers added more and more problems to the teacher's list. We listened to their problems attentively and sensitively. Then we asked them whether anything was working in the community. We asked them to focus for a moment on the village's assets, its capacities, the pride of its residents, the cooperative and institutional base of the community, not on what might be absent, or problematic, or on the community's needs. To our surprise, the mood changed to one of laughter and celebration as the villagers, one after the other, narrated the good news stories of the proud people of Kagera.

In the Mombo area development program in the Northern Zone the project coordinator uses an adaptation of the 4–D model. In December 1997 Northern Zone staff joined the Mombo project coordinator to facilitate a workshop attended by area leaders focusing on capacity indicators to assess their ability to plan, carry out and evaluate their self-development. This process involves seven steps.

1. During a relationship-building time, people are encouraged to share their good news stories, their strengths and opportunities, their dreams and their shared visions.

2. Communities compare existing situations with the desired and preferred future. Focusing on similarities and differences between the community vision and the actual situation helps establish baselines.

3. Communities determine what capacities are required to achieve their vision. What habits, skills, knowledge, attitudes and values are required in a particular community for it to achieve the vision? Often, communities with the greatest capacity to change do not possess certain knowledge and skills, but do possess spirit, enthusiasm and hope for transformation. Most communities choose to build capacity in management, spiritual values, finance, networking and technical areas such as health and agriculture. The community itself establishes capacity goals.

4. Using the plant cycle as a metaphor (planting, germination, growing, fruit/flowering and propagation), communities are challenged to evaluate their level of maturity in selected skills. By assessing its level of capacity in each area, the community establishes capacity baselines from which to build.

5. The community develops specific indicators in each category toward the phases or stages of its growth. These indicators will help the community monitor and assess progress on a regular basis. How does a particular community know it has moved from planting in relationship-building to germination and to growing? Community capacity indicators help give the community signals of making, or not making, progress.

6. The community formulates strategies and plans to systematically build its capacity to achieve the desired future. These strategies and plans are developed through participatory processes that enable men, women, youth and children to be part and parcel of the vision.

7. An outside agency such as World Vision becomes a facilitator, empowering communities through developing local capacity to a point at which community members graduate and become independent of the agency.[15]

A workshop focused on identifying capacity indicators on a matrix (see Figure 3–4). Participants were instructed, "Using the matrix, put an X in the appropriate box to indicate where the area development program and the community are in each type of capacity they are building in order to achieve their vision." They identified specific indicators to decide what constitutes *growing* in management and leadership, *planting* in finance and fund-raising, *planting* in networking and partnerships, *planting* in technical areas (health, education, agriculture, water), and *germinating* in spiritual/kingdom values. These participants felt good that they were making some progress in two types of capacity and felt challenged to do more in finance, networking and technical areas.

Phases of area development program	Management / leadership	Finance / fund-raising	Networking / partnerships	Technical areas	Values / spiritual
Planting		X	X	X	
Germination					X
Growing	X				
Fruit / flowering					
Propagation					

Figure 3–4: Identifying capacity indicators.

To summarize, indicators facilitate determining what capacities are required to achieve a community's vision. Community partners develop indicators that enable us to contract with them on progress toward sustainable development and eventual "graduation" from partnership with us. This spirit of learning with our partners has led us to commit ourselves equally to staff and organizational capacity building.

STAFF CAPACITY BUILDING

We like to say that staff are our most important resource. In the last three years our management has tried to introduce an encouraging environment built on the following principles:

Appreciation: We are committed to appreciating staff members and upholding their contributions to our ministry. We want to celebrate their respective gifts and talents and enable them to worship God through their work. We acknowledge that each staff member is created in God's image and that our job is to let him or her shine for Jesus.

Empowerment: We are committed to empowering staff members to be the best they can be by maximizing their skills and abilities toward a higher quality of ministry. We want to develop staff to increase the overall value they add to our ministry.

Competitive benefits: We commit ourselves to competitive salaries and benefits in comparison with our peers in our local environment. We strive for fewer but higher-paid staff who are capable of greater contributions to our ministry.

Stewardship: Recognizing that our resources are not our own but have been entrusted to us, we are committed to acting responsibly and with high integrity regarding compensation. We encourage a transparent and clearly understood human resource strategy that builds ownership and commitment from all staff.

These principles have helped to build staff capacity and increase overall morale. Examples of how this has been implemented include the following:

Positioning: We have made a specific attempt to develop a horizontal organizational structure, in contrast to vertical thinking (see the section on organizational structure below). Staff positions are organized into categories of similar positions in terms of job responsibility and overall value to the ministry. A "position matrix" outlines expectations for each position and indicators for performance and competency. Staff work together not only to build individual performance but also team performance. And staff now have more opportunities to be "promoted" within their categories as opposed to waiting (perhaps indefinitely) to move up the ladder. Morale increases when staff members feel valued and appreciated by management.

Performance appraisal: Positive feedback encourages staff members, who in turn build stronger more effective organizations. Using a format that includes all those around a staff person (supervisor, peers and support), our appraisal procedure is designed to highlight "best practices." Rather than using a scoring system, performance is illustrated by the agrarian model used in many communities (see Figure 3–4). This model attempts to do away with the practice of rating performance by numbers, substituting growth indicators. Emphasis is on development for greater performance and thus higher value to ministry. Staff who have used the format feel more encouraged and less threatened by this appreciative, constructive process, and the format has led to more focused training for staff capacity building.

Training: We have developed a comprehensive staff-development policy designed to provide staff with the necessary skills, knowledge, abilities and attitudes to achieve our mission. A participatory training program includes staff member and organization in a contractual plan for developing agreed-upon capacities. The policy seeks to celebrate and build on proven capacities within staff and develop these further for even higher performance. Priority is given to developing women at all levels within the organization. Two exciting examples are:

- *Accredited development studies:* In the East Africa region, we have begun an education program that will grant up to a master's degree from a recognized university in the United Kingdom, utilizing distance learning and modules taught by accredited professionals in the field. At present there are seven students in the program, with an additional seven entering in October 1999.

- *Capacity-building associates:* Given the facts that we seek to hire well-qualified staff (both academically and experientially) and that most university graduates in Tanzania have limited experience, we have established an intern program. For one year, university graduates can build field experience within our programs. Participants, who are provided with a living stipend, receive an appreciative action/reflection/action learning experience designed to qualify them for future positions in development organizations.

ORGANIZATIONAL CAPACITY BUILDING

One of the most important ingredients to the whole process of Appreciative Inquiry in our office has been developing an encouraging management and leadership style.

We encourage managers and leaders to:

- See challenges and opportunities instead of problems.
- Identify positive potential in every person and situation.
- Respect and value uniqueness and individual differences.
- Communicate recognition of individual movement, progress and contributions.
- Communicate openly and honestly.

- See themselves as equal to others in worth and dignity, and therefore to treat supervisors, colleagues and subordinates as equal participants in the process.
- Provide positive performance reviews.
- Communicate in a language of equality through collaboration, cooperation, agreement and "win-win" relationships.
- Facilitate open communication of short- and long-term company goals or mission statements.
- Commit to giving and receiving feedback.[16]

Management and leadership must model this style if we expect others to follow.

Organizational structure

We present our structure as a horizontal set of networks and relationships, as opposed to a hierarchical structure, pushing accountability as close to the level of implementation as possible. Focus is on functions (or cross functions), not on positions. Teams are the critical component. Such an organizational structure promotes and celebrates the contribution of each member and team as a valued part of the whole. Accountability and ownership for results has allowed us to decrease overall staff while at the same time doubling our ministry.

Board development

A local board of trustees to whom management is accountable governs our work. An AI approach to board development includes focused training programs, sharing of reading materials, site visits, participation in partnership events and involvement in local program activities. Our board's capacity and contribution to our ministry have greatly increased, and trustees dedicate one extra day each meeting time for board development activities.

Fund-raising

As part of our overall mission, we set a goal of increasing our ability to attract and harness local funds for development programs. Last year we raised 15 percent of our total budget locally. This year the goal is 25 percent. We use a unique fund-raising strategy developed by Jim Lord and based on AI.[17] Our premise is that fund-raising is not so much a process of raising money as it is of providing opportunities for involvement. Our focus is more on the donor than the donation. Our goal is to provide to the donor rich experiences that lead to transformative commitments. This approach has worked well with individual donors as well as major bilateral and multilateral donors.

LEARNINGS

We have learned much from our AI/capacity-building journey.

- Appreciative Inquiry is not so much a tool or a methodology as it is an attitude or approach. It is very flexible and can be used in many different situations. Persons using AI should seek to contextualize the basic principles for their own needs.
- Basic assumptions of AI (that is, that image and action are linked, that we move in the direction of the questions we ask and that the best practices of the past lead to best opportunities of the future) have proven true in the process of community development.
- Capacity building requires organizational, community and staff development. The synergistic relationship of these three components leads to holistic capacity building.
- To develop capacity in others, an organization must be involved in a process of internal capacity building. Development organizations must reflect the same transformational changes that they hope to promote within local communities.
- Organizations and communities develop at different speeds and at different levels. An evaluation process that identifies critical indicators of capacity and helps to identify priorities for growth should lead to mutual accountability, managed regularly through commitments and reporting.[18]

FUTURE PLANS

In 1999 we will be conducting a workshop for leaders in government, NGO and donor communities. Our goal is to get others excited about this great opportunity for developing capacity.

A few people have wondered whether Christianity and AI are contradictory. We think not, and in fact we argue that they are complementary. We would like to do more study in this area and show how AI can be used as an effective Christian witness and nurturing process. AI is still a relatively young concept and needs continued research and development.

Notes

[1] Paulo Freire, *Pedagogy of the Oppressed* (New York: Seabury Press, 1970).

[2] James Mayfield, *Go to the People* (West Hartford, Conn.: Kumanian Press, 1985), 157.

[3] B. J. Lecomte, *Project Aid: Limitations and Alternatives* (Paris: Development Centre of the Organisation for Economic Cooperation and Development, 1986; USA distributor: Washington, D.C.: OECD Publication and Information Center).

[4] Hans Dieter Seibel and Andreas Massing, *Traditional Organizations and Economic Development: Studies of Indigenous Cooperatives in Liberia* (New York: Praeger, 1974).

[5] Freire, *Pedagogy of the Oppressed*, 57.

[6] David C. Korten, "Community Organization and Rural Development: A Learning Process Approach," *Public Administration Review* (September/October 1980), 480–511.

[7] Rose Loretta, "Investigating AI: A Handbook of Readings, Reflections, and References for the 1998 WV West Africa ADP Managers' Workshop," San, Mali (March 19–27, 1998), 9–10.

[8] Liebler, C. J., "Getting Comfortable with Appreciative Inquiry: Questions and Answers," *Journal of Global Social Innovations* 1, no. 2 (Summer 1997), 30–40.

[9] Sarone Ole Sena and Dirk Booy, "An Appreciative Inquiry Approach to Community Development: The World Vision Tanzania Experience," *Journal of Global Social Innovations* 1, no. 2 (Summer 1997), 7–12.

[10] Caroline Sahley, *Strengthening the Capacity of NGOs* (Oxford: INTRAC, 1995).

[11] David Cooperrider, "Positive Image, Positive Action: The Affirmative Basis of Organizing" (1992).

[12] The "Miracle and Mystery" section was adapted from Christian Reformed World Relief Committee (CRWRC), *Partnering to Build and Measure Organizational Capacity* (Grand Rapids, Mich., 1997).

[13] Piet Human and André Zaaiman have developed a similar model when describing organizational effectiveness (see *Managing Towards Self-Reliance* [Capetown, S.A.: Phoenix Pub.; Senegal: Goreé Institute, 1995]).

[14] CRWRC, *Partnering to Build and Measure Organizational Capacity*.

[15] Ole Sena and Booy, "An Appreciative Inquiry Approach to Community Development."

[16] Don Dinkmeyer and Daniel Eckstein, *Leadership by Encouragement* (Delray Beach, Fla.: St. Lucie Press, 1996), 8.

[17] James Gregory Lord, *The Philanthropic Quest* (Cleveland, Ohio: Philanthropic Quest International, 1995).

[18] For an earlier list of critical learnings, see Ole Sena and Booy, "An Appreciative Inquiry Approach to Community Development," 9.

Our Experience with the Bible and Transformational Development

Joy Alvarez, Elnora Avarientos and Thomas H. McAlpine

THE SHALOM VISION

Shalom ("sustainable peace" or "harmony within diversity") is first God's vision and then our vision for the world. It is the reign of right relationships, where God rules over the created order. The creation account in Genesis portrays a blueprint of God's intention for life as it should be: harmony between God and human beings, harmony within each person, harmony among persons, and harmony between human beings and nature. Metzler describes such harmonious interaction and fulfillment as an incredible paradise:

> Eden's shalom was perfect because everything was just the way God made it—connecting the possibility of shalom directly to the creative powers of God. Out of the primeval chaos, void, and darkness the Creator had planned and formed an orderly and purposeful world. ... The Creator looked over that work with complete satisfaction: "Behold, it was very good" (Genesis 1.31). Shalom affirms that the truly good life is the natural state for all creation, and that all creation is truly good, with a place and purpose for every part. ... The shalom of all creation depended on the man and woman using their godlike powers of choice. ... The shalom of Eden ... pointed to the need for community and companionship (1985, 60–61).

Though the Fall brought an end to shalom, resulting in alienation and disharmony in the created order, the "God of shalom" never gave up. "If shalom is life as God made it, then shalom is life as God still intended it to be. Yahweh embarked on a grand mission, stretching across the ages to restore that original vision" (Metzler 1985, 61). The unifying, oft-repeated theme from the Old Testament to the New Testament is that the God of Creation is on a mission to restore shalom, calling a special people to be in communion with God, recipients of God's blessings and agents of shalom.

Jesus Christ modeled the shalom ministry. Summing up his mission as preaching good news to the poor, proclaiming freedom for the prisoners, recovery of sight to the blind, releasing the oppressed and proclaiming the year of the Lord's favor (Luke 4.18–19), there was perfect consistency among Christ's words, deeds and life. He preached, lived and demonstrated shalom.

Transformational development

Transformational development is an expression of the mission of shalom. It is the act of responding positively to God's call to be partners with God in rebuilding the kingdom. Transformational development seeks to respond to the needs of the poor in a holistic manner. It seeks to follow Christ in the way he went about doing his ministry, encompassing the physical, spiritual, social and cultural dimensions of personal and societal life. It hopes and works for change in people toward the ideal of the kingdom of God as demonstrated by improved relationships with God, self, others and the environment.

The strategies and approaches of transformational development affirm the dignity and worth of people as created in the image of God. People and communities are challenged to define their own vision, and manage and own the development process as planners, implementers, evaluators and change agents themselves. Recognizing that the roots of poverty are complex, transformational development nonetheless seeks to enhance people's awareness and ability to free themselves from the cultural, social and spiritual bondage that causes them to remain in poverty, oppression and unjust relationships. The manner by which this will be done will be consistent with the character and activity of a loving and just God. It will be redemptive, nonviolent and seek reconciliation. Poverty is not simply an economic imbalance but also oppression by principalities and powers holding the poor captive. Not only must interventions employed be technically appropriate, sustainable and of high quality, but we should also rely on committed Christian staff, prayer, Scripture and the power of the Holy Spirit.

Transformational development: Let the buyer beware!

Development

Even with the best intentions (or perhaps precisely because of them) we acknowledge the highly problematic character of development, whether due to pluralism in values or the seemingly inevitable negative side effects of technology, modernization and urbanization. The Argentinean cartoonist Quino and the Mexican poet and essayist Octavio Paz are two Latin American witnesses to this problematic. Octavio Paz writes:

> Progress has peopled history with the marvels and monsters of technology but it has depopulated the life of man. It has given us more things but not more being.
>
> Let us look at what is happening in the United States and Western Europe: the destruction of the ecological balance, the contamination of lungs and of spirits, the psychic damage to the young, the abandoning of the elderly, the erosion of the sensibilities, the corruption of the imagination, the debasement of sex, the accumulation of wastes, the explosions of hatred. Faced as we are by all this, how can we not turn away and seek another mode of development? . . .
>
> It is an urgent task that requires both science and imagination, both honesty and sensitivity; a task without precedence, because all of the modes of development that we know, whether they come from the West or the East, lead to disaster (Paz 1972, 8, 46–47).

Why is this important? To the degree that the communities with which we work have not begun to understand this, there is little felt need for any reflection, let alone the participation of Scripture in an integral way in our work. In these contexts, if Scripture is used, it is characteristically to "baptize" project activities or to introduce themes that communities perceive as unrelated to project activities (for example, evangelism).

Promoters of development

We are increasingly aware of the profound ways in which development promoters themselves affect—for good or ill—the development process. Thomas Merton provides exemplary articulations of this point.

A Trappist monk in Kentucky, USA, Thomas Merton ministered through his letters and writings to the world, whether in the inward journey ("spirituality") or in the outward journey (mission, including political engagement). He wrote:

> He who attempts to act and do things for others or for the world without deepening his own self-understanding, freedom, integrity and capacity to love, will not have anything to give others. He will communicate to them nothing but the contagion of his own obsessions, his aggressiveness, his ego-centered ambitions, his delusions about ends and means, his doctrinaire prejudices and ideas (Merton 1971, 164).

If we are not self-consciously pursuing our own transformation, then our use of Scripture will rarely be other than self-justifying. One might say it is inevitable that Christians will use the Bible in ministry; the interesting question is whether using the Bible will reveal Christians to be lords or servants of Scripture.

Scripture

God creates and re-creates—gives life—by his powerful Word. We have experienced the Bible to be life giving. The words of Ezekiel's audience ("Our bones are dried up, and our hope is lost; we are cut off completely") are often echoed in communities with which we work. Thus we return to hear again Ezekiel's account of his vision (Ezek. 37). He is brought to a valley full of dry bones—and told to prophesy to them.

> So I prophesied as I had been commanded; and as I prophesied, suddenly there was a noise, a rattling, and the bones came together, bone to its bone. I looked, and there were sinews on them, and flesh had come upon them, and skin had covered them; but there was no breath in them. Then he said to me, "Prophesy to the breath, prophesy, mortal, and say to the breath: Thus says the Lord GOD: Come from the four winds, O breath, and breathe upon these slain, that they may live." I prophesied as he commanded me, and the breath came into them, and they lived, and stood on their feet, a vast multitude.
>
> Then he said to me, "Mortal, these bones are the whole house of Israel. They say, 'Our bones are dried up, and our hope is lost; we are cut off completely.' Therefore prophesy, and say to them, Thus says the Lord GOD: I am going to open your graves, and bring you up from your graves, O my people; and I will bring you back to the land of Israel. And you shall know that I am the LORD, when I open your graves, and bring you up from your graves, O my people. I will put my spirit within you, and you shall live, and I will place you on your own soil; then you shall know that I, the LORD, have spoken and will act," says the LORD (Ezek. 37:7–14).

The point of departure and the point of return is not the Bible as a source of rules or a conceptual foundation (although it may function in these ways), but as a mediation of the creative power of our God, the ultimate basis of our life and ministry. This is something that differentiates Christian development from secular development. Scripture gives hope, life, dynamism and immense possibilities beyond human imagination. This makes reflection upon Scripture critical to human transformation. At the same time, our reflection must be self-critical, which entails being clear about our assumptions.

Assumptions

How we use Scripture reflects our assumptions regarding Scripture, people and community, our role as an organization, as well as a methodological option for diversity.

Scripture

Within the Western Christian tradition we tend to assume that:

- Scripture is primarily addressed to the individual.
- Scripture is primarily about spiritual things.
- Scripture is primarily about the world to come.
- Scripture is primarily written from the divine point of view (McAlpine 1995, 69–70).

The Scripture Search method (along with other methods we focus on here) represents a fundamental reorientation in the assumptions we often bring to Scripture:

- Scripture is primarily addressed to the community (and therefore to the individual-in-community).
- Scripture is about all spheres of life (and therefore also about the spiritual).
- Scripture is primarily about this world (and so, by extension, also about the world to come).
- Scripture is primarily written from the divine point of view, which is also the view from among those who are "the least of these who are members of my family" (Matt. 25:40).

What we are dealing with is the ongoing struggle against a dualistic mindset in ourselves and others, a mindset that divides reality as follows:

Spirit/soul	Body
Church (religion)	State (politics)
Faith	Reason/science
Private morality	Public morality
Sunday	Monday-Saturday
Evangelism	Development
My work for the church	My work for the organization

Figure 4–1: A dualistic view of reality.

Within the dualistic mindset the Bible can only be heard and interpreted as speaking about the column on the left. That the Bible presents the gripping narrative of God's attempt to construct in human history societies that will not self-destruct—an attempt that has a great deal to suggest about how we promote development at the grassroots—disappears from view. Engagement with the preceding understanding involves using both specific studies (text- or theme-based) as well as more global efforts at reorientation (for example, Steward 1995).

The project community and its members

Speaking from the Philippine context, Mac Bradshaw identified several assumptions regarding God's work in community life, which influences all our uses of Scripture:

- God is already at work in a community before we even come on the scene.
- Community members have accumulated a great deal of wisdom about a variety of topics, including spiritual perspectives on life.
- The community must take responsibility for its own spiritual pilgrimage, rather than simply adopting a pre-planned one from elsewhere.
- People in community can make their own application of spiritual truth to their local situation.
- World Vision's presence in a community is not the sole source of the community's Christian nurture. Local churches have a major responsibility for contributing to the community's spiritual nurture (in McAlpine 1995, 71–72).

For both principled and practical reasons we seek to facilitate transformational development so the communities with which we work are viewed as subjects, not objects: principled, because otherwise we deny the community's dignity; practical, because otherwise project activities may be irrelevant to local realities and people may rightly regard this as our problem, not theirs. If the community is subject, then the community must be able to read and reflect on the Bible and not simply consume the reflections of others.

Affirming the community as subject highlights the importance of the action-reflection-action process. We must emphasize the dialogue regarding community commitments, values, beliefs and traditions. These elements will influence project possibilities in positive and negative ways. If the community does not reflect on these elements, it can easily lose its soul in the rush toward modernization. The action–reflection–action process is an important place for this dialogue.

To speak of Bible readings in the context of action–reflection–action indicates that readings are part of regular meetings of already-established groups. The point is not to generate new groups. Working with this cycle, the Bible serves in the moment of reflection to illuminate our past and guide our future. Bible readings are not something isolated but part of the normal processes of development.

Genesis's description of humankind as bearing the "image and likeness" of God and the apostle Paul's image of the body of Christ teach us to value and seek the contributions of all. Therefore we seek meetings in which all can contribute and are not satisfied when cultural patterns limit speech to the leader—or to males. The value of participation implies seeking ways of reading in which all can participate.

There is also a missiological motive for paying close attention to participation. We frequently encounter situations in which we do our development work participatively but use the Bible in non-participative ways. People's experience and perspectives really matter, it seems, if the subject is education, health or water . . . but not God. The danger is that our methods will witness to two "gods": the "god" of development, who values human participation, and the "god" of Scripture, who devalues it: shut up, listen, obey! Our choice of method powerfully determines what we communicate.

The organization's role

And what is the development agency's role in the development process? According to Bradshaw, the "charism is probably more that of people discovering the King by gradual acquaintance of His ways through experiencing His reign in specific issues/problems of living, the experience being interpreted by their own search of an appropriate Scripture case alongside their experience. Other charisms, such as that of evangelistic outreaches, are more fitting to overt 'church growth' than is the development process" (in McAlpine 1995, 72).

The following text from Jeremiah suggests a parallel approach to this question:

> Then they said, "Come, let us make plots against Jeremiah—for instruction shall not perish from the priest, nor counsel from the wise, nor the word from the prophet. Come, let us bring charges against him, and let us not heed any of his words" (Jer. 18:18).

Jeremiah's announcement assumes three traditional sources of guidance for a community. If we ask where what nongovernment organizations bring to communities fits within this typology, the answer would appear to be counsel. This applies also to our use of Scripture. We read Scripture with communities not as priests or prophets but as learners. The wisdom orientation toward tolerance and universality gives us the freedom to read Scripture with folk from a variety of traditions.

Diversity

No one method responds completely to the variety of contexts within which we work. We need methods appropriate for small groups and large groups. We need methods that allow us to bring our questions to the Bible, as well as those that allow the Bible to bring its questions to us. That is, we need methods that move in the Bible-to-life direction as well as in the life-to-Bible direction.

In this chapter we focus on two methods: from the Philippines, Scripture Search, which normally uses studies moving in the life-to-Bible direction; and from Latin America and the Caribbean, the Seven Steps, a reading (not a study), moving in the Bible-to-life direction.

It is worth recalling at this point that the challenge for our work is more than methodological. Married to an unrepentant dualism (see above), the best methods will lead us astray. Married to our own will to power (our desire to be served by rather than to serve Scripture), the best methods will simply serve as new ways of proof-texting.

THE PHILIPPINES

What is Scripture Search?

The basic question Christian development staff faced was how community development work could be holistic and Christ-centered. The answer that emerged was to focus development on Scripture—not so much in a doctrinal, religious mode, but rather to see the world in terms of transforming the daily life of the individual, family and community. Thus Scripture Search is a way of integrating Scripture into the transformational development process. These are some of Scripture Search's specific characteristics (drawn from Bradshaw and McAlpine [see McAlpine 1995]):

1. It is deliberately nonsectarian and non-proselytizing in character. It is a way that invites Jesus himself to come and walk with people as they talk with each other about everything that has happened (Luke 24:14–15), to explain "to them the things about himself in all the scriptures" (v. 27), and even to open eyes to recognize him (v. 31). It gives people the opportunity to urge Jesus to "stay with us, because it is almost evening and the day is now nearly over" (v. 29).
2. The facilitator, who may be a project staff member or community member, comes prepared to introduce a Scripture reading during the reflection period, when experience-sharing is at a high point. Preaching or teaching on the text is discouraged. The story or verses chosen are handled like a case study in the case-study method of learning.

3. The people themselves discover the relevance of Scripture to the issues they are wrestling with. Facilitators use questions and other methods to draw out insights and participation.
4. There are three fundamental questions:
   a. What are the similarities between experience in biblical times and our experience now? (This leads to contextualization.)
   b. What light does that experience cast upon our current experience? (This leads to prayerful reflection.)
   c. As individuals and as a group, what should we do about these insights? (This leads to actualization.) This question forms a bridge to new plans for group action, helping to ensure that Scripture is lived obediently and practically. Obedience or non-obedience is accounted for in the next meeting.
5. Facilitators find that selecting appropriate Scripture stories is easier if positive and negative values and attitudes emerging in the group's experience are identified. The subject matter of group reflection (self-esteem, servant leadership, conflict, commitment) normally does not touch on dogma or the specifically "religious" but focuses instead on values recognized as relevant to everyday life.

Scripture Search and human transformation

Communities testify that their journey toward change often starts through the use of Scripture Search in the development process.

Men, women and children

First, Scripture Search allows individuals in community to experience personal change. Positive results include:

- A deepening relationship with God.
- Improved family relationships.
- A stronger commitment to serve others through community leadership roles.
- Children showing more respect for parents.
- Youth participating in community activities.
- Community leaders gaining confidence to lead.

Families

Alice Oreanza has grown in her understanding of Scripture through her involvement in Scripture Search with a project in Zambales, northern Philippines. Having had unhappy experiences of attending Bible studies that ended in heated debates and broken relationships, Alice initially felt some resistance to Scripture Search. She discovered, however, that Scripture

Search spoke to her and helped her cope with problems she faced as a community leader.

Alice once felt very discouraged and was at the point of giving up her leadership role because of severe criticism from some people in the community. Then she felt tremendous encouragement at the next Scripture Search session she attended. She began to read the Bible by herself when she was at home. After completing her chores, she would sit quietly in a corner and read the Bible while the rest of the family members went about their activities. After doing this regularly, her husband asked, "How about reading aloud, so we can hear as well?" Not long afterward, she discovered her husband reading the Bible; soon her children followed suit. They had never been a regular church-going family, but now they are. Alice feels that these activities have led to stronger family unity.

Because of the impact of Scripture Search in her life, Alice wanted others in her community to share her experience. Now she is active in organizing Basic Christian Communities and using Scripture Search in these communities.

Communities

Doray is now the first and only councilwoman in her village. Her entry into politics was influenced by a Scripture Search session focused on the Isaiah vision (Isa. 65:17–25), which was the vision of the core project group working in the community. She was so taken by the Isaiah vision—which speaks of children not dying, the elderly living full lives, people building houses and living in them, planting and enjoying the fruits of their labor and being in harmony with God—that she adopted it as her political platform. She became the first woman elected to the village council, long dominated by men. Believing that politics and the Word of God can go together, she always insists on something that was never done in council sessions: opening and ending meetings with prayer. She now shares the Isaiah vision with her peers on the council, hoping it will become the vision of the whole community. She is working to introduce Scripture Search in the council, as well as other critical processes that will help facilitate development in the community.

Building partnerships with churches

Scripture Search is not meant to be the only tool for integrating Scriptures in the community. The role of the church is vital as well; local churches need to carry out the church's mandate to nurture its flock in the community. Synergy is most likely to happen when there are good relationships between the development organization and the local churches, both Catholic and Protestant. Mistrust and suspicion can be a deterrent to broader community participation and can prevent the church's participation in a potentially catalytic people-empowerment process.

When World Vision began development work in southern Cebu province, the community welcomed the team of project workers who came to live with them. Hopeful that the development process would improve their quality of life, a core group formed quickly to do community projects. Scripture Search became a regular feature of their meetings. But not everyone in the community was happy about this. A devout Catholic couple, Paz and Eddy, held back their involvement and suspected that proselytism was part of World Vision's agenda. They spoke with the parish priest, who warned his parishioners against participating in community activities organized by World Vision.

The moment for reconciliation came when the core group organized a Catholic Lay Evangelization seminar with trainers from the Institute for Pastoral Development (IPD), a Manila-based Catholic training institute in Scripture study, evangelism and holistic methodologies. The institute is the training ministry of Joy of the Lord Community, the oldest and largest of the Catholic charismatic groups in the Manila archdiocese. The core group invited Paz and Eddy, who joined 15 other participants for the five-day evangelization seminar. Paz and Eddy were soon going house to house, sharing the gospel with their neighbors. Soon after, the couple began attending community meetings where Scripture Search was being done.

The project team's reports and efforts to build a relationship with the parish priest gave him reason to apologize for his warnings about World Vision. He has since become a staunch ally and has encouraged expansion activities in new communities.

Building houses and living in them

The Isaiah vision (65:17–25) has helped people see that God's intent for their lives is holistic; it encompasses the whole of life as individuals living in the context of family and community. Manang Mencia of Mangaco, a community in southern Cebu, was so captivated by this vision she began dreaming she would eventually redeem her land, which for 20 years had been pawned to a moneylender. She boldly approached the project facilitator, who brought her case to the core group responsible for managing the development project in the community. The core group, inexperienced in dealing with such situations, reflected on the Isaiah vision and decided to help Manang Mencia by giving her a loan. Manang Mencia has since repaid the loan in full. There are many others who have had similar experiences.

A squatter community in Davao City has realized its dream of owning the land where its members had been under the constant threat of eviction. Through a committed organized group, diligent planning, implementation and monitoring, prayer, networking, Scripture Search, a compelling vision, a strong dose of patience and persistence and the presence of a facilitator, the group overcame the many difficulties that stood in the way of achieving its goal.

Approximately thirty families in Cavite, who lived in makeshift shanties in a cemetery, were relocated to a new community. This became possible through the efforts of the community's core group, which sought to make Isaiah 65 a reality. The strong links the group had with government councils made it possible for the mayor of another town to open doors for the relocation of the families.

Learnings that facilitate wholeness and transformation in people and communities

Besides introducing Scripture Search as a critical tool for community change, the development organization can benefit from using Scripture Search extensively in its own activities, integrating Scripture with organizational processes and initiatives. The following represent important principles that have evolved from organizational use of Scripture Search.

The Bible is a text on transformational development

The modern world often treats the Bible as a religious book used for isolated "sacred" reading, irrelevant to "secular" life. But our work with communities has led us to rediscover the Bible as a powerful story explaining the meaning and purpose of life, full of cases that model abundance, reconciliation, forgiveness and the transformation of persons, communities, nations and nature itself.

The Bible provides a powerful vision of hope for the world

Scripture presents a captivating vision of a new humanity, a new heaven and new earth; indeed, a new world, a new creation. Prophets and apostles warn of a purifying judgment followed by the original creation made perfect according to Jesus' vision of shalom. Revelation 21–22 speaks of an eternal New Jerusalem, the kingdom of God consummated. Isaiah 65 speaks of the ultimate kingdom partially realized in the present world.

The Isaiah vision (65:17–25) has become a powerful poetic picture that captures the imagination of the poor. Serving as a graphic picture of a bright future, it mobilizes community groups to action.

Paradigm shift toward kingdom values

The prevailing missiological paradigm of the conservative Protestant churches in the 1980s often limited Christianity to individual conversion and Sunday involvement with the local church. Donald Kraybill's *The Up-side-down Kingdom* proposed a new paradigm. Kraybill points out that Jesus ushered in the kingdom of God, the dynamic rule or reign of God (Kraybill 1978, 20). An illustration of how upside-down kingdom values differ radically from the world's values is how Jesus redefines greatness. Contrast Jesus' use of "greatness"—bottom, servant, slave, last, child—with the world's definition of "greatness"—top, powerful, master, first, ruler, adult (Kraybill 1978, 243).

The "How" of people empowerment

Eleven years ago, after resolving that the poor should be the focus of our ministry in the Philippines, the next critical question was how we were to do this. Would we empower the poor themselves or empower other community groups (the local church, government agencies)? Some argued that the latter would involve fewer capacity-building efforts. But our reflection on Isaiah 61—which talks about the poor as primary actors in rebuilding and restoration—strengthened the conviction that empowerment efforts should focus on the poor themselves.

> The spirit of the Lord God is upon me,
>   because the Lord has anointed me;
> he has sent me to bring good news to the oppressed,
>   to bind up the brokenhearted,
> to proclaim liberty to the captives,
>   and release to the prisoners;
> to proclaim the year of the Lord's favor,
>   and the day of vengeance of our God;
>   to comfort all who mourn;
> to provide for those who mourn in Zion—
>   to give them a garland instead of ashes,
> the oil of gladness instead of mourning,
>   the mantle of praise instead of a faint spirit.
> They will be called oaks of righteousness,
>   the planting of the Lord, to display his glory.
> They shall build up the ancient ruins,
>   they shall raise up the former devastations;
> they shall repair the ruined cities,
>   the devastations of many generations (Isa. 61:1–4).

The process of capacity building was not simply skill-focused but aimed at building self-confidence and the inherent capacity to dream and to mobilize collective efforts to build a better quality of life. At the core of the empowerment process is the need for the poor to have a growing awareness of their disempowerment and the web of realities that conspire to relegate them to poverty. The spirit of empowerment occurs when the poor recognize that God is supreme over all powers vying for the poor's allegiance and discipleship. God is the power that fuels a community's efforts to unshackle itself from the chains of poverty, oppression and injustice. This experience of freedom is empowerment, a blessing. The process becomes even more dynamic when the empowered (the blessed) desire, seek and work so that others will likewise be empowered (be blessed). Empowerment becomes the "mustard seed" that grows to be a big tree giving shade and rest; it can scale up and gain momentum to become a strong people movement.

Blessed to bless others: Making the Abrahamic covenant our own

When God called Abraham to leave his country and people and become the father of a great nation, there was promise of great blessing. However, God did not intend this blessing for Abraham alone. It was meant to bless other people as well.

"I will bless you . . . so that you will be a blessing. . . . And in you all the families of the earth shall be blessed" (Gen. 12:2–3).

Those who have had long experience in development know that at times the process of empowerment can simply reverse the status of the poor from victims to oppressors. The cycle of poverty stays in place; only the players change. For Christian development organizations the Abrahamic covenant becomes a source of hope to break this cycle. The poor experience God's blessing, and in a gesture of gratitude to the Giver, share their blessings with others who are even poorer. They recognize that they are blessed so that they can bless others.

Living as a people with a mission

We discovered the best way of carrying out our mission among the poor was to pattern our work after Jesus' example in Luke 10:1–12: live among the poor, participate in their community life and proclaim shalom. Our development teams went to live among the poor; their lives and relationships became open books to the communities with which they worked.
The next important consideration was how to have an organization that lives and breathes its mission. According to Matthew 9:16–17, if we put new wine into old wineskins, the old wineskins will burst. Providentially, we were given the opportunity to turn old wineskins into new. What ensued were organizational processes to align and attune our strategies, structure, management style, corporate culture and policies with our shared mission and core values. Having the whole organization walk and talk the vision

was powerful; it unleashed tremendous energy and concerted action. Both the communities where we lived and worked and our staff were captivated by the same vision.

Challenges

The development facilitator's lack of confidence

The facilitator's ability to integrate Scripture Search into the development process contributes to a project's success. New staff must be coached by seasoned team members on the use of Scripture Search. Inexperienced staff assigned to a new community are often confronted with other concerns, making it easy to relegate Scripture Search to something "that can be done later." Indefinite postponement does not help the facilitator gain the confidence he or she needs in using the new skill.

Staff who lack discipline and desire for deeper study of Scripture

Staff who experience fulfillment in doing Scripture Search invest much time in the study of Scripture. But not all staff members have time and motivation to do this. Only to the extent that Scripture Search becomes a way of life for staff will it be integrated into the community's life.

Failure to document the richness of the community's discoveries

The failure to document experience has been repeatedly recognized not only as an individual staff weakness but as an organizational weakness as well. Although a documentation guideline is available, facilitators rarely find the time to document after community meetings. The process and learnings during Scripture Search sessions are usually not captured.

Future directions for Scripture Search

Our experiences with Scripture Search encourage us to anticipate much more in the future.

Agents of change experience transformation themselves

The facilitator or change agent is critical to the Scripture Search process. Beyond the skills necessary to prepare and facilitate Scripture Search is a spirit of discernment to sense deeper issues people are grappling with.

R. J. Salsalida, the facilitator who tested Scripture Search at its inception, remarks, "I always benefit first from the Scripture Search process." Through the years, Salsalida has developed the discipline to study and share

Scripture with others. The passion to study Scripture must go with the passion to apply it to one's life and experience.

Contributing a vision of holistic ministry to local churches

Local churches must join the community in overcoming the bondage of poverty. Robert C. Linthicum captures this vision:

> That church becomes flesh of the people's flesh and bone of its bone. It enters into the life of that community and becomes partners with the community in addressing that community's need. That means the church allows the people of the community to instruct it as it identifies with the people. It respects those people and perceives them as being people of great wisdom and potential. Such a church joins with the people whom they have identified as their own . . . recognizing that the only people who in the final analysis have this capability to change the community and to deal with its problems are the people of that community (Linthicum 1991, 23).

In seeking to have churches espouse such an attitude toward their communities, we dream of churches drawing nearer to Jesus, who was usually found among a community's poor and marginalized. In serving the poor, churches draw nearer to one another. We desire our church partners to have (1) a vision for holistic ministry; (2) a vision for serving with the poor; and (3) a vision for unity in the body of Christ.

People becoming community

The ultimate goal is that the communities we serve become praying, sharing and caring communities. This is identical to our intention for our own staff. This calls for advanced training in the Scripture Search method. As more facilitators increase their commitment to and skills in Scripture Search, more communities will have opportunities to experience the power of the Word to influence and change their lives.

People's organization leading to people movement

Becoming a people movement is a long-term goal. The image is of a wave created by tossing a pebble into a pond. A single stone will create ripples that grow in ever-enlarging circles, at times connecting with other ripples to make even larger ripples. We have formed People's Congresses, grand gatherings of stakeholders from around the country, occurring every few years. These are times of celebration and worship, as well as times to build unity and address common concerns.

LATIN AMERICA

Included among a range of Scripture and community development methods is the Seven Steps, a variety of participative studies for small groups, and the *pastoral popular,* a methodology developed in Brazil for socializing biblical themes with large groups. There is an increasing number of studies on particular themes (for example, studies on women and men in leadership, and studies dealing with micro-enterprise development).

The Seven Steps

The Seven Steps is a Bible-reading method developed by the Lumko Institute in the Republic of South Africa. It is an adaptation of *lectio divina* (divine reading) for use in small groups attempting to respond to community needs.

Although we often think of Bible reading as primarily a mental exercise, people in biblical times experienced it as something more intimate. One of Ezekiel's visions captures this well:

> He said to me, O mortal, eat what is offered to you; eat this scroll, and go, speak to the house of Israel. So I opened my mouth, and he gave me the scroll to eat. He said to me, Mortal, eat this scroll that I give you and fill your stomach with it. Then I ate it; and in my mouth it was as sweet as honey (Ezek. 3:1–3).

In the first centuries of the church's life experience with the Bible began to be spoken of in terms of four movements: reading, meditation (thinking or reflecting over the text), contemplation (experiencing God's presence beyond words) and prayer. In practice, the believer is easily moved among these different movements, going, for instance, from reading to meditation to reading to prayer to meditation to contemplation, and so on. Somewhat later this practice received the name *lectio divina.*

The Seven Steps, then, is a method of Bible reading, not of Bible study. It emphasizes group listening and receptivity rather than an active group search for literal meaning. It is oriented by the question, What does God want to say to me? rather than, What does God want us to do? Nevertheless, the shared weakness and vulnerability that this question implies, and the practice of patient listening it nurtures, translate powerfully (as we see below) into an increased capacity to address development project concerns in a group ethos of peace and receptivity.

William Stringfellow helps us recall the importance of such listening:

> Listening is a rare happening among human beings. You cannot listen to the word another is speaking if you are preoccupied with your

appearance or impressing the other, or if you are trying to decide what you are going to say when the other stops talking, or if you are debating about whether the word being spoken is true or relevant or agreeable. Such matters may have their place, but only after listening to the word as the word is being uttered. Listening, in other words, is a primitive act of love, in which a person gives self to another's word, making self accessible and vulnerable to that word. It is very much like that when a person comes to the Bible (Stringfellow 1994, 169).

The context indicated for use of The Seven Steps is a stable small group in a project or church setting. *Stable* means that basically the same people are in each meeting. (It can be used with illiterate groups as long as one person can read.) The texts most appropriate for this method are the Gospels and Psalms.

The method

Figure 4–2 provides an overview of the method. Here are some additional comments:

Read. The facilitator announces the verses, but only after all have found the chapter in the text, for the participation of every person is important.

View with wonder. The point is not to identify the most important word or phrase but rather the word or phrase that touches or beckons one. Thus this step is about listening and responding.

Listen. Participants continue to lis-

The Seven Steps

1. Invite
We remind ourselves that the Risen Lord is with us. Would someone like to welcome Jesus in a prayer?

2. Read
Let us open our Bibles to . . .

3. View with wonder
We pick our word or short phrases, read them aloud prayerfully, allowing enough silence between them to say the words three times in our hearts.

4. Listen
We keep silence for ___ minutes and allow God to speak to us.

5. Share
Which word or phrase has touched us personally? (Do not discuss any contribution.)

6. Group tasks
Now we discuss any task or work our group is called to do and report back on our previous task. What new task needs to be done? Who will do what and when?

7. Pray
Anyone who wishes may pray spontaneously. We close with a hymn, chorus, or prayer that everyone knows.

Figure 4–2: The Seven Steps.

---

ten, now in silence. The recommendation is not to use the time for active prayer or meditation but simply to remain in and enjoy Jesus' presence.

Share. Participants may share how a word or phrase of the text has spoken to or illumined some part of their life. Preaching or arguing about the text is discouraged.

Group tasks. The group now focuses on its tasks, for example, those of a group of health promoters or the project's leadership. The text read in the second step normally does not have a thematic relationship with these tasks. Nevertheless, the practice of careful listening in the previous steps characteristically influences the way participants approach their tasks and their relationships with each other.

Positive results

The following results have been reported regarding the use of the Seven Steps method:

- deepening of individual relationships with God
- improved teamwork in general
- participation of both Catholics and evangelicals
- reconciliation among participants
- improved behavior of participants outside of the meetings
- increased participation in local churches

Some observations of participants in El Salvador include the following:

- It's a simple method within reach of everyone, independent of the person's educational level.
- It promotes participation.
- It can be used with groups containing people from different churches.
- It's not useful for proselytizing but achieves direct contact with the Word (the Bible) and God.
- It's a method that needs much humility on the facilitator's part, because the Seven Steps don't permit an exhibit of the facilitator's knowledge.
- The attitude of the participants should be that of prayer. They too need humility so the biblical text can resonate in their lives.

The above-mentioned aspects determine whether the participants in the small groups experience little or much satisfaction with the method.

Issues

In most of the contexts in which we work, the dominant way of using the Bible has been authoritarian—the authority declares what the Bible says. The participants may never have experienced using Scripture in group settings other than by preaching or exposition on the part of the leader. In this context the temptation is strong for the center of gravity to shift to the fifth step of the Seven Steps process and for that step to become a forum for preaching.

Facilitators who are unfamiliar with a variety of participative ways of using Scripture may use the ones they know in inappropriate ways. Some areas have used the Seven Steps to facilitate thematic studies or large-group meetings. This points to the need for familiarity with a wider range of methods.

Again, dualism may appear as the Seven Steps are redirected toward producing individual conversions—or as facilitators feel guilty for not so redirecting the process! Nevertheless, these issues exist only because there is openness and a desire to learn on the part of staff.

Frontiers

Methods

Our current and developing practice puts us in a position to continue learning regarding both Bible-to-life methods (Seven Steps, some Bible studies) and life-to-Bible methods (such as Scripture Search).

Beyond this, one open question is the place or role of more intensive Bible-to-life studies. The power of such an approach was evident in Bangladesh in the early 1980s. The director had been facilitating a series of inductive studies in the Gospel of Mark with Muslim staff. A situation arose in which the office had to choose between supporting a community it had been working with or accepting a government decision that could prove harmful to the community. Since that choice might well have implications for staff, the director asked the staff what action they would take. Their response: we think this Jesus we've been reading about would support the community; that's what we want to do.

Church relations

Our search for appropriate ways of reading Scripture in the context of development projects is one of a number of activities highlighting the need for more intentional and strategic relations with the churches. This is true from two perspectives. First, using Scripture in projects is sustainable only if project agents engage in regular personal Scripture reading and receive formation regarding Scripture from some local expression of the church. Second, development projects have a great deal to do with money and power. Scripture has plenty to say about how we deal with these elements, regarding them as fundamental questions for discipleship. This provides an obvious opening for conversations with the churches: We're trying to help project leaders read Scripture in ways that will empower them to make better choices regarding money and power. How is this connected with what you're doing? Where can we learn from you or build on what you're doing?

Development as lectio

To move from seeing development as the transfer of money or technology (predefined solutions for predefined needs) to seeing it as a participative process in which the people are subjects, not objects, is progress to be celebrated. But we have not fully achieved our goal. The Seven Steps *(lectio)* rhythm of read, meditate, contemplate and pray may help us deepen our practice in two ways. First, the emphasis on silent receptivity can help us see our reality more clearly. (There are important affinities between *lectio* and Appreciative Inquiry.) Second, emphasis on silent receptivity, starting with Scripture but potentially extending to other "texts," can create space for us to ask what God has been doing in our communities, what gifts God has given us, what hopes God might have as to how those gifts might be used and for whom.

RECAPITULATION

What we've seen

Scripture, used participatively, is playing a vital and irreplaceable role in community development projects, addressing individual and group values and behaviors, uniting (rather than dividing) Christians from different traditions. In the Philippines, where participative methods have had a chance to mature, Scripture has become a major motor for institutional learning and transformation.

Our experience suggests that over time we should encourage a variety of methods in a particular context: methods that emphasize listening/contemplation/receptivity (such as Seven Steps) as well as those that emphasize reflection/meditation/creativity (methods in the direction Bible-to-life as well as life-to-Bible).

Next steps

We must continue to expand our "tool kit" of participative ways of reading the Bible among ourselves and with communities. This means continued attention to the possibilities of Bible study within project contexts. It means identifying and developing ways of hearing the Bible's story as a whole—so that its holism is not lost. It means attention to nonlinear and non-print-based ways of passing on the content of the Bible. It means attention to the variety of challenges posed by working in settings that do not have a Christian tradition.

We need to continue to give attention to sustainability, for the various creative initiatives regarding Scripture and holistic mission have not yet reached critical mass within development organizations. This includes areas such as staff formation, more adequate documentation of our experiences and increased communication.

And we must improve church relations to maximize possibilities for joint learning and formation. We still have a great deal to learn. We have staff at all levels who badly need contextualized formation. The good news is that we do not have to do this alone, and to the degree that we can work out what this means in practical terms, we and the whole church will be better for it.

Bibliography

Kraybill, Donald. 1978. *The Upside-down Kingdom*. Scottdale, Pa.: Herald Press.

Linthicum, Robert. 1991. *Empowering the Poor: Community Organizing Among the City's "Rag, Tag and Bobtail."* Innovations in Mission. Monrovia, Calif.: MARC.

McAlpine, Thomas. 1995. *By Word, Work, and Wonder: Cases in Holistic Mission*. Innovations in Mission. Monrovia, Calif.: MARC.

Merton, Thomas. 1971. *Contemplation in a World of Action*. Garden City, N.J.: Doubleday.

Metzler, James E. 1985. *From Saigon to Shalom*. Scottdale, Pa.: Herald Press.

Paz, Octavio. 1972. *The Other Mexico: Critique of the Pyramid*. Translated by Lysander Kemp. New York: Grove Press.

Steward, John. 1995. *Biblical Holism and the Missionary Mandate*. Sydney Centre for World Mission and World Vision Australia.

Stringfellow, William. 1994. *A Keeper of the Word: Selected Writings of William Stringfellow*. Edited by Bill Wylie Kellermann. Grand Rapids, Mich.: Eerdmans.

PART THREE

OUTCOMES

5

Discovering a Role in God's Provision

Sustainable Economic Development for the Church and the Poor

DAVID R. BEFUS

ECONOMIC DEVELOPMENT
AND THE CHURCH

A new missionary venture begins with an "emphasis that every Christian is a missionary and should witness through his daily vocation." "Missionaries work in exchange for their travel to the field, and all field expenses are paid out of indigenous income." Economic activities are considered "a trust from God, an aid toward fulfilling the tasks of the church, and a source of employment and community life" for the church.

These quotations are from the story of missions in North America more than two hundred years ago, as documented by William Dankar in *Profit for the Lord*, published in 1971 and now out of print. Dankar describes how the Moravian Mission began its outreach in Pennsylvania in the 1700s with a strategy founded on economic development and small enterprise. He also chronicles the economic activities of the Basel Mission Trading Society, and how business and trade were used as a tool to support church outreach in Africa and India.

Church outreach has often been connected to economic development. A foundation for knowledge about this connection might include academic research and field experience. This chapter is based principally on my own 25 years of experience working in various contexts to promote economic development in developing countries. Cases cited are events that actually happened.

Principles and practice: Cases to help understand the fundamentals

*God as maker and human beings made in God's image: FIME community
banks in Santo Domingo, Dominican Republic*

"In the beginning God created," we read in the first book of the Bible,
and we are told that God worked, and rested from work. Human beings,
created in God's image, also worked, overseeing God's creation. Humanity's
work was part of the rhythm of the universe, even before sin entered the
world. And provision for material needs is directly related to work. Once
sin entered the world, productive activity took on another dimension, requiring toil and effort. But the basic pattern of provision in relation to labor
continues to this day.

As churches consider ways to reach out in ministry, some have used the
creation of work opportunities as a basis for creating relationships. The
FIME development loan program in the Dominican Republic has provided
loan capital to dozens of community banks that were organized by churches,
providing a means for the church to respond to neighborhood needs for
income generation. From a ministry vantage point, the church uses a development tool—the community bank—as a bridge or channel to the neighborhood. As one pastor said, "Most of the people here would never have
entered the church door, because they find our singing and talking strange.
But they came to the church to participate in a program to generate family
income and gradually became part of our church as well. Even if they do
not attend Sunday services here, we consider them part of the family, and
we pray for them and take an interest in their well-being."

This pastor is also the treasurer and a board member of the community
bank. His church is located in Tres Brazos, an urban squatter town on the
outskirts of Santo Domingo. The community bank currently has 65 members, and a revolving loan capital of US$17,800. Members of the bank meet
monthly to evaluate the bank's individual and collective progress. Their
meetings include opportunities for biblical reflection and personal sharing.
Many business problems are actually symptomatic of spiritual problems,
and in this regard the church context provides full services, with counselors
and prayer, as well as administrative and technical assistance. There are 21
community banks organized in churches by FIME, some of which are in
Barahona and Jimani, very poor areas of the country.

The methodology appears to benefit the lending organization as well as
the church, as the church-organized groups have very low arrears and good
reporting mechanisms. From a service-delivery perspective, church members actually perform, on a voluntary basis, many administrative functions
critical to overseeing loan programs. This also means that such programs
can provide very small loans and still be financially sustainable. This is a
win-win proposition: the church obtains a valuable tool to help people in

the neighborhood generate income, and the lending organization gains access to volunteer services that allow it to reach the poor with very low supervision costs. The net result responds to people's material needs by promoting productive activity, enabling men and women to work, as God intended.

Old Testament principles and Jehovah-jireh, God our provider: CARITAS Juticalpa helps the poor help themselves

God is known to us in many ways, among them, God our provider. God's provisions generally do not come by magic or miracles, but through productive economic activity. In the Old Testament we generally see God's provision through agricultural production that requires work. The specific principle is presented often in Proverbs: "Those who till their land will have plenty of food" (12:11; 28:19). It is also presented by the writer of Ecclesiastes: "So I saw that there is nothing better than that all should enjoy their work, for that is their lot" (3:22).

Teaching this principle in our churches is often accompanied by the painful realization that, in practice, there are many other factors that affect God's provision for us. Some factors can be addressed only by prayer. Others, such as access to land, capital, markets or production technology, may require assistance. As they say in Honduras: *A Dios orando, con el maso dando* (we pray, and at the same time we keep hammering away).

The CARITAS program in Juticalpa, Honduras, is an example of how the church has addressed the economic challenges facing church members. The nine parishes that are within a 100 kilometer radius of the city of Juticalpa, an agricultural hub, can access loan funds for small agricultural projects, women's or men's groups, and young people and families. Interest is charged on the loans to cover both costs of operation and devaluation. Most of the loans are for agricultural production, focusing on investments that provide cash payment rather than on consumption crops.

This program has impressive financial statistics, but even more important is its integration with other programs for health and spiritual and community development that address holistically the needs of the poor. It also includes technical training to improve seed varieties, implement organic and environmentally safe methods for control of insects and use of fertilizer, and storage and marketing techniques to improve profit margin.

There are similar attempts by CARITAS Honduras to address problems in other cities. For example, in Tegucigalpa there is a network of community banks that function in similar fashion to the FIME program described above. The success of the CARITAS economic programs in Honduras has provided the basis for the church to present a funding proposal to the Inter American Development Bank to expand these programs, not only in Honduras, but in the rest of Latin America.

New Testament principles and instructions to "work with your hands":
Juan XXIII furniture project in a Costa Rican slum

The apostle Paul's statement in 1 Thessalonians 4:11–12 is quite clear: "Aspire to live quietly, to mind your own affairs, and to *work with your hands*, as we directed you, so that you may behave properly toward outsiders and be dependent on no one" (emphasis added). Paul repeats the same principle in Ephesians 4:28: "Thieves must give up stealing; *rather let them labor and work honestly with their own hands*, so as to have something to share with the needy" (emphasis added). Work is not only critical for providing for one's needs, but is also key in helping others.

These texts, however, are little used by churches in developing countries, because unemployment is high and there are no jobs. The priest or minister who uses this as the sermon text risks the obvious question: How do we put this into practice? Such was the situation in the squatter town of Chapulines, Costa Rica, when a Bible study and social needs survey was promoted by Escuela Juan XXIII and implemented by university missionaries associated with Latin America Mission. The survey indicated that the majority of heads of households were women, sole supporters of their children, and their major need was for income to provide for their families. But they were unemployed and unable to leave their homes in many cases.

The response was a project to make bean-bag furniture, based on sewing that could be done within the home. Economic-development literature calls this a *sectoral approach*, but the missionaries and university student volunteers knew nothing of this; they were only trying to find a way for the women to work with their own hands and not be dependent on anybody. Prototype models were made, raw materials purchased and market outlets defined. The project was very successful, and many women also began making other products that they sold on their own. Gradually, management of all of the business activity was transferred to the women, without outside support. Addressing the community's economic needs changed the Bible study atmosphere and deepened relationships with the church.

Latin America Mission continues to integrate economic activities with mission outreach. Its ministry to children is supported by a poultry business, and it operates a vocational school in a squatter village to create income opportunities for the poor. These and similar projects are tools that support and promote evangelistic outreach.

Tent-making to "offer the good news free of charge":
A Nicaraguan evangelist

It is interesting to note that the early church had problems due to its social assistance program, which some members perceived as welfare for freeloaders. There were arguments about distribution of assistance (Acts 6:1). Paul is clear in his second letter to the Thessalonians that welfare freeloaders are not welcome: "Anyone unwilling to work should not eat" (2 Thess. 3:10b). He presented himself as a model. He was a craftsman and, as we know from Acts 18, made durable portable housing—tents, but unlike our concept of camping tents. He promoted a model of sustainable self-reliance, even though he acknowledged his right to donated funds. It was common practice for rabbis or teachers to have a skill to generate income so that they would not be completely dependent on revenue from their students. The skill Paul had in making tents enabled him to generate income to support himself when needed.

Instructions to work for a living had special significance to those involved directly as leaders of Christian ministry. Paul recognized the right of those in ministry to request offerings, but he did not take offerings for his own ministry; he felt his message would be more credible if "I may make the gospel free of charge" (1 Cor. 9:18).

Pastor Julio felt God's call to be an evangelist, but could not leave the church where he was ministering because he needed the monthly salary, and he knew that evangelists earned barely enough to pay for room and board. He heard about a loan program run by a Christian organization, and he applied for a loan to start a ceramics business. He had investigated the business and believed it would be a great "tent-making" opportunity, because he already had experience making plaster-of-paris Bible verse plaques, which he sold to bookstores.

The loan was invested in a small kiln and working capital. He taught his daughters how to make the clay, fill the molds and heat the kiln. In a few years he was able not only to support his ministry but also to expand his business with a bigger kiln and the full-time involvement of his children.

A variation on this approach is being used by missionaries in countries where there are restrictions on the open presentation of the gospel. In China a missionary organized a decorative glass factory, which exports a high quality product and employs 60 people. He is not allowed to directly present the gospel, but he can respond to questions and discuss spiritual matters with employees. A church has been started through this outreach. In Mauritania a missionary operates a loan program that has helped many people increase their income and has also provided a social context for all of them to hear the gospel. A small church has also begun there, and a few individuals have decided to follow Jesus. Both of these programs also generate revenue, but the more important aspect is that they allow for a credible Christian message in a context where direct evangelization is not permitted.

Solidarity with the Carpenter who said, "Give us this day our daily bread"

Jesus worked for many years in his father's business. Because Jesus was the oldest son, some scholars believe he may have run the family business for many years. That Jesus knew the world of business is apparent from his statements and parables. The actual business he was in goes beyond simple woodworking, as the Greek word for carpentry is used for construction activity that includes masonry and general construction. His story of the "wise man building his house on the rock," and the statement in Luke 14 about "which of you, intending to build a tower, does not first sit down and estimate the cost," indicate our Lord's own experience as a building contractor.

Jesus' understanding of the world of productive activity in his time was not restricted to the construction business. He speaks of workers unhappy with their pay, of employees who know they are going to get fired and use their last days on the job to prepare, of the handling of loan funds, and tells many other stories based on experiences from the world of business. He recites the fundamental outcomes of farming, explains how herding sheep works, demonstrates an understanding of tree farming, and shows knowledge of the fishing business. Jesus was well acquainted with many of the fundamental productive activities of his day.

God provides for people through productive economic activity. Since the beginning of time people have had to work to support themselves. Welfare assistance or miracles occurred from time to time in response to specific needs: manna in the desert, the widow's jar of oil, and the loaves and fishes. But these were the exception; in general, people earned their daily bread through productive economic activity. This has been the plan since the creation of the universe, was evident in the example of God-made-flesh, and is God's plan for us today.

POTENTIAL AND CHALLENGES OF CHURCH INVOLVEMENT IN PROMOTING ECONOMIC DEVELOPMENT PROGRAMS

The potential of economic programs for outreach, support and sustainable development

There are many ways to envision the process by which communities and people can promote sustainable development. For example, the practice of washing hands, boiling water and using a latrine may represent a sustainable pattern that offers great benefits to people. In the same way, there may be sustainable patterns of community organization and sustainable improvements in agricultural practices that affect the environment.

What people and communities want, at some point, is to confront the issue of economics. One thing the poor have in common is a lack of money. This may not be the first issue to address in community development. Health, community organization and education may provide a foundation for productive activity. But once the basic foundation of social services exists, most people want to do something productive to support themselves and meet their needs. Often community projects require surveys and forums to determine what a community needs, and the issue of economics generally comes from community leaders, not necessarily from social workers or church workers. Women who are single providers for their children often identify the need for additional income in many contexts. Rural-urban migration is related to the need for employment. Unless there is work, people move to other places, generally to the city.

A great advantage of church-related programs is that financial services can be integrated with other development interventions as part of a total package to address the needs of a poor community. Unlike many churches, other organizations that promote loan programs do not have ways to access community groups, build on existing educational and health services, or combine financial services with other community programs.

What about gifts and donations as a foundation for transformational development?

A traditional response to community interest in economic programs has been to provide production inputs on a donation basis. In some contexts the donation is considered much more acceptable than a loan, not only because it appears to be consistent with donated funding, but also because it is possible to donate to people in an equitable fashion. Since there are no requirements, everyone is eligible. For example, many health projects offer primary care volunteers "income-generating resources" as an incentive, without regard to entrepreneurial interest or ability of the health volunteers.

There is also a related approach of providing "loans" but not really requiring that they be paid back. Much funding for economic activity in church and relief organizations continues to be either donated or channeled to soft "loans" that are not tracked in relation to payback. Beneficiaries of these programs see them as short-term windfalls. In some cases business activities are funded by donating assets or productive inputs rather than cash; these assets can then be sold or liquidated, or in many cases the entire production is consumed without regard to additional productive cycles. For example, with food production, there may be project controls over the initial investment in planting, but no controls over what is done with the actual harvest.

Studies done in many organizations, and in the public sector, have consistently identified basic problems with the gift/donation approach to economic activity:

- the underlying businesses funded are generally not viable;
- the donation is not valued;
- the lack of discipline creates great incentives for fraud and mismanagement.

It is for these reasons that this type of project is criticized. There is now recognition that if potential clients must present plans to make a net profit, there is more likelihood that there will be funds generated to reinvest in the continuation of their productive activity. It is also recognized that soft-loan programs have actually taught people that they do not have to keep financial commitments, thereby limiting their possibilities of accessing resources from other sources in the future.

Perhaps the most damaging of the three problems is the fact that enterprises funded with donations are generally not viable in the marketplace. Expectations are created, and the poor experience yet another failure. For example, dozens of women are taught to sew and provided with cloth, machines and thread. But concern for quality output, response to markets and adequate pricing are not included in the training. Once the sewing course is over, the photos taken and the budget spent . . . nothing remains except the memory of another failure. The donor agency can easily absorb the loss even if the machines disappear, but what about the people who thought this would help them support their families?

The church as an administrative foundation for economic program service delivery

The cases presented earlier in this chapter involve a clear separation between the church and the economic program service delivery. Previously, loan programs have been a source of fraud in communities, especially if there was little or no tracking of what happened to the loan receivables, whether paid or unpaid. Individuals who do not pay must learn the lesson that loans have to be paid and promises kept. Funds invested in the program cannot be stolen or somehow disappear but must be managed with integrity and professionalism. To prove this is so, economic programs generally are run separately from church programs.

Managing economic programs through separate entities also helps protect the church. Delivery of economic services is held at arm's length, and decisions on whom to help do not fall to the clergy. The need to promote collection of loans does not mix with spiritual and religious counsel, nor confuse motivations of laity, when performed by a separate entity.

Models for institutionalization of economic development programs

Managing loan or business creation programs requires supervision and controls—and clear ownership definitions. A separate, sustainable entity is required to institutionalize financial services for the poor and to guarantee a disciplined system for recycling benefits after the initial intervention is completed. This special entity may or may not be registered as a legal parallel organization, but it must be allowed to have its own management system and focus on its specific mission.

The church and its programs can function as a precursor for economic development programs. For example, training activities might take into account the need to prepare people for productive activity in the real world economic environment. If the church funds small experimental projects for training, specific boundaries should be drawn in relation to beneficiary expectations, and the concept of graduating to a sustainable level of production should be encouraged. Technical training that promotes innovation and product quality should be encouraged, and loan programs should support graduates of this training.

There are three specific levels for promoting sustainable economic development, beyond the subsidy or "hidden handout" stage.

1. The first stage is to guarantee that funded proposals are *viable projects* in the real marketplace.
2. The second is to demonstrate defined procedures, client lists, receivables tracking and reports that indicate that a formal *service delivery program* exists.
3. The third stage is the presentation of financial reports that show how costs are covered by revenues in a *financially sustainable* pattern. A parallel entity, a legally registered organization with separate management, has proven the best mechanism to attain these goals and to serve the target population on a sustainable basis.

MICRO CREDIT PROGRAMS AS A BRIDGE BETWEEN THE CHURCH AND ECONOMIC DEVELOPMENT

Micro credit as a development tool

Governments of most countries support micro credit as a development strategy. It is one policy that generally has support from politicians on opposite sides of the ideological spectrum.

The Grameen Bank and other large micro-enterprise development (MED) programs have eloquently presented the argument in favor of micro credit as a development tool. The poor want a "hand up, not a hand out." They are capable of managing loan funds on a very small scale and paying them back. The cost per job created in the "informal sector" is far lower than the formal sector, and micro credit can address the pressing needs of those in the lowest economic levels.

Church-related programs may offer additional benefits. Such programs may include integration with holistic community-development programs and target populations that are generally poorer than those of other micro-enterprise development agencies. They may take risks that others do not take, for example, in financing rural agriculture. They promote direct and indirect Christian witness along with financial services, recognizing the importance of the invisible world alongside the visible. They access other services for training and supervision from other church or parachurch structures. They also may be organized at very low costs due to existing administrative infrastructures.

World Vision's experience in creating and nurturing new MED institutions

In five years World Vision in Latin America has created 17 loan entities with US$7,000,000 in revolving loan funds. Except for two, all of these entities are legally registered parallel organizations, with national boards of directors and close cooperation with World Vision's national offices. More than half the programs already cover all of their costs, and the others have targets for arriving at financial sustainability within the next two years. The programs must be financially sustainable, as they are not allowed access to national office budgets to cover their overhead.

Most of these programs were organized with three-year targets for sustainability based on US$300,000 in loan capital. Eight of the 17 programs have more than US$500,000 in loan capital. Except for the Peru ASODECO project, which is part of a USAID project, all programs were weaned from external special-funding support after two years; special funding was regarded as temporary and passed on to the next new program.

The potential with the Latin America loan fund is to rotate it twice per year, because the average payback period is six months. The programs can now provide an additional US$14 million annually in resources for helping the poor. One outcome that has been measured is job creation and strengthening. In 1998 the programs created 1,141 new jobs, and strengthened 4,867 existing full-time jobs. Another outcome is training for productive activity. Also in 1998, 227 training workshops were held for 4,226 clients, over half of whom were women. Training involves direct Christian witness, supplementing witness opportunities Christian staff have while supervising client projects in a Monday-to-Friday context.

The impact of World Vision's micro-enterprise development programs has been especially great for women, who are often the sole providers for their families. Women comprised 64 percent of funding in 1998, not because there is any specific program that discriminates in favor of women, but rather because they tend to be more responsible than the men in paying back their loans.

Barriers to expansion of church-related economic development

Despite the successes mentioned above, some World Vision national offices have rejected the micro-enterprise development concept because they do not believe there is sufficient community participation in this type of program. Though communities generally participate in client selection and even board membership, this is considered insufficient participation. In some cases, restricting loans to those who have viable projects is considered unfair. Sometimes national offices are unable to provide management support for the concept. At other times the idea that the "community should make its own decisions" has been carried to the point where the national office does not wish to or cannot exert a leadership role. The separate, specialist concept of micro-enterprise development financial services does not appeal to some managers or national directors, as it takes resources out of their ultimate control: funds deposited for loan capital cannot later be accessed for operating expenses or invested in other types of programs.

Some of these same tensions exist in CARITAS Honduras and have resulted in difficulties in presenting a national proposal. The commitment to disbursement and collection policies that will make a national program sustainable has been controversial, as not all the national offices want to implement the same systems or even require the same interest rate. The application process for securing additional funding for loans has therefore been delayed, as these issues are negotiated internally.

A common barrier to success with micro credit start-ups is accepting discipline in relating costs to revenue. The tendency is to fill in the expense budget without filling in the loan disbursement requirements. This must not be allowed, or expenditure patterns will eliminate any possibility of the program eventually becoming sustainable. This issue illustrates the fact that loan programs must be managed with a business mentality and thus may require a different administrative culture than church organizations. Sustainable revolving-loan programs are actually small banks, and they must be managed like banks.

What remains in a community when the development intervention is over? This is a critical issue to address when plans are developed to promote income and employment. The advantage of the separate, sustainable, specialist approach to promote economic development is that it will continue even when church programs and emphases change. The economic programs can therefore attain sustainable levels and be one truly visible sign of involvement in helping the poor.

There are also ideological barriers to economic activity related to the church. The Bible is clear about the dangers of the love of money, but money and business, since business operates with money, are sometimes also viewed as evil. Add to this negative image of economics the worries about capitalism, exploitation, risk and possibilities for fraud and stealing, and many church managers would rather not get involved in economic programs. This is another argument for creating economic programs in entities separate from the church, with their own distinct management. It also may explain why so little is written about integrating economics with church activities: perhaps it would not be well viewed by supporters and donors.

THE CHURCH'S FUTURE ROLE IN THE DEVELOPMENT CONTEXT

Doing good and doing it well

Helping people to succeed in "working with their own hands" is a ministry. It is part of the testimony of Christians, for whom doing good is a sign of God's kingdom. The apostle Paul's letter to Titus mentions "doing good" eight times as the sign of the Christian. Micro credit programs are a wonderful opportunity to do good.

Doing good also means doing a good job: "Whatever you do, in word or deed, do everything in the name of the Lord Jesus" (Col. 3:17a). Church organizations must approach economic goals for their members and other people with a concrete definition of micro-enterprise development, adequate performance standards, competent management, responsible means of governance, and evaluation and reporting systems. They need to do this because they want to do the best job they can.

Anticipating the church's context in developing countries in the next century

The goal of long-range success implies short-range complications. One critical problem in implementing disciplined micro credit programs is that they require a complex management system. It is much easier simply to give things away; all managers ask for is a receipt to show that goods were purchased. But when you lend funds, you need to know how those funds will be used. You need to train people to use the funds in a productive manner, so that revenue from the business, and not further indebtedness, is the source of the payback. The funds must be collected, and then channeled to someone else. These technical activities are what make the program work. Most development practitioners realize that complex problems require complex solutions. This is what makes development work so challenging. Those who work in micro-enterprise development have all the complexities of big business . . . and none of its resources.

The global marketplace has broken down protectionism, and the small producer also must compete internationally. The price of shoes in the market in Tegucigalpa is affected by the cost of raw materials in Brazil and labor rates in China.

There are wonderful new opportunities for the small producer to participate in international trade and gain access to markets that were never before anticipated. The knitted miniature soccer ball made in the Guatemala highlands can become a hit product in the United States and employ hundreds of women.

International standards for currency valuation have fallen, and the trend toward deregulating economies seems to put all countries at the whims of the world financial system. This has brought a new type of vulnerability to international economic fluctuations, which is felt at all levels.

It has been said that the economy of the future will be based on what one knows, not on what one does, and the small producer should also be allowed access to new technologies that are critical to maintaining competitiveness. But rural areas of the developing world are a long distance from urban areas and have little to no chance of connecting to the electric grid, the telephone network or the Internet.

A call for a serious response from the church in a global future

Can the church play a role in helping the poor to compete in the global marketplace? Can the church help the poor to find market outlets for their production? What role does the church play in economic development? How can the church help?

The church has a special ability to promote economic activity that is also development oriented by connecting micro-enterprise development to community development projects. But a strategic vision must now emerge for economic development as a worthy program in its own right, a ministry that is allowed to grow in meeting the needs of the poor to obtain their daily bread by working with their own hands.

World Vision says its organizational mission is "to follow our Lord and Savior Jesus Christ in working with the poor." This means we should seek to have the mind of Christ in discovering constructive roles to promote our mission. The writer of Hebrews said Jesus shared fully in our experience in living here on earth, including the workplace (4:15). Our Lord knows what it is like to manage a small business. His hands were just like the hands of the poor whom we serve. May these same work-roughened hands guide us, as we seek new ways to obey, honor and give God the glory.

6

Community Organizing
and Transformation in an Urban Context

Daniel Ole Shani

THE PLACE

Descending for landing at Nouakchott International Airport in the late afternoon, I looked to my right through the plane window. I could just see through a haze of dust a haphazard mixture of tiny houses and makeshift tents as far as the boundary of the shifting yellow sand dunes of the Sahara Desert. I had seen this same scene from the air at least a half dozen times since my arrival in October 1996. For airplanes landing at Nouakchott, flying over this part of the city was the usual line of approach before descent. This was Arafat, home to more than 100,000 residents, a refuge of sorts here on the edge of the capital city of the Islamic Republic of Mauritania. Mauritania's huge land mass of 1,085,760 square kilometers is home to a total population of only 2.2 million people. Almost all of them live in the more hospitable southern one-third of the country.

In the early 1960s many migrated to Nouakchott, capital of the newly independent Mauritania, lured by work opportunities created with the construction of a modern city on the edge of the Atlantic Ocean, where desert and sea meet. This influx increased Nouakchott's population from an estimated 5,000 people in 1959 to 25,000 in the mid-1960s.[1] From the mid-1960s to the beginning of the 1970s, Nouakchott's population more than doubled to 55,000. Harsh droughts in the mid-1970s led to further migration surges and drove the population from 55,000 to 104,000.[2] People continued to trickle in from rural areas until the next drought cycle in the 1980s, which increased the population to more than half a million by the end of that decade. Some scholars referred to Nouakchott at that time as "the largest refugee camp in Africa."[3] Currently, Nouakchott's population is estimated at 700,000, almost one-third of the nation's population. Forty percent of

94

these 700,000 live in squatter settlements, of which Arafat is the largest, with more than 100,000 people. This is where World Vision, an international Christian organization that has been working in Mauritania since 1984, started the Road of Hope Urban Program in 1994, to enable residents of this settlement to overcome barriers to their own development.

Municipal authorities divided Arafat into seven sectors, but roughly 70 percent of the people live on land not yet surveyed or allocated. This land is called *gazra* in Hassaniya Arabic, widely spoken in Mauritania. Arafat's earliest residents have lived on the land since the mid-1970s. At that time only a few tents sat scattered on the sand.

Poverty in Arafat is not strikingly evident to the casual observer. The sand can obscure, from a distance, the relative squalor of houses. The common manner of dressing—robes called *boubou* for men and either colorful full-length veils for Moor women or colorful print clothing for Pulaar and Soninke women—disguises whether people are able to clothe themselves adequately. Water, transported from pipes[4] to the *gazra* areas in drums mounted on donkey carts, is available. Latrines are not common, but plenty of deep sand and dry weather take care of the rest. Food is plentiful in shops. So why get involved in Arafat?

Adult illiteracy was a major factor. In 1994, 66 percent of Arafat adults were illiterate, and of the women, 79 percent were illiterate. One man described his illiteracy, saying, "I was just like an animal. I wasn't a person really. The difference between an animal and a human being is the mind, the ability to think. . . . I have tried two times to open a shop and failed. I lost my money because I could not do arithmetic."[5] Thousands in Arafat were in a similar condition.

Another factor: "Squatters" living on the *gazra* lacked a sense of community. Their perception was that they were powerless to speed up land allocation or participate in municipal development planning.

A recent study by the German Technical Cooperation agency captured the community's hierarchies: The "rich" poor eat three meals a day. They include some meat in their diet every other day. They can often afford to rent a cement-block house. But much of their income comes from illicit activities. Then there are the "piece work" poor. They are on the streets each day looking for temporary work here and there. They can afford two meals a day and often live in a homemade shack. But they can't afford school fees for their children or required notebooks. Finally, the "poorest" poor hope for enough from alms and other handouts to feed themselves. They live in threadbare shelters. Among all three strata are many female-headed households.

Traditionally, Mauritanians have a strong sense of family kinship relationships but not a strong sense of community. In traditional nomadic family units, immediate family (sharing the same family name, in addition to the nuclear family) was counted on for resource sharing and social exchanges.

The idea of people from different ethnic groups and families collaborating together was foreign. Associations were rare, not cohesive and lacked clear objectives. A strong community-wide network was needed to influence municipal decision-makers. Child sponsorship funding, begun in early 1998, provided a fresh opportunity to create a community network founded on a clear common interest and objective. Mothers of the 600 sponsored children, representing all ethnic groups, organized themselves into three groups of 200 each. From each group, the mothers elected 20 representatives to a grassroots committee. This committee of 60 mothers then elected 21 mothers to a coordination committee. This committee now deals directly with World Vision to design poverty alleviation strategies and represents the 600 families when dealing with government and other local leaders on Arafat development matters.

Accurate unemployment statistics were not collected during the initial stages of the work in Arafat. Based on the 30 percent unemployment rate in Nouakchott and our project's random surveys, however, it is quite certain that many able-bodied people were underemployed and unemployed. The ability to purchase food, clothing and water is severely limited, not by availability, but due to residents' low income levels and the relatively high cost of these items. Water costs more for the poor, since those who sell it must first buy it from a piped water installation. Typically, loans for the poor were impossible to secure from commercial banks, which did not consider them credit-worthy, despite the common observation that Mauritanians are, for the most part, very enterprising people, able to start and run small businesses effectively.

Nena Mint El Voulanij was exactly the sort of person to whom a commercial bank would not lend money. She was married at 12; at 13 delivered her first child, who died soon after; divorced for the first time at 15 after having her second child; and remarried shortly after that. She moved with this husband from their rural community to Arafat in 1981, and very soon thereafter her second husband abandoned her and their three young daughters. She met six other single mothers like herself in her neighborhood, and together they formed a small cooperative that produced the traditional full-length veil called a mehlafa *worn by Moor women. Business was good for a while, but as the group grew to 25 members, they soon found they often lacked enough cash to buy fabric and dye at wholesale prices. They learned about Road of Hope Urban Project and eventually took a loan for US$1,433 from the project's micro credit unit. In just over a year the women were able to boost production and incomes to a point of repaying the loan in full while being able to care better for their families. They qualified for a second loan of US$1,470, which they invested in their business. To date, they produce and sell to other women the veils that they sew, tie and dye.*

"Before World Vision's credit program began here in Arafat, women like Nena had good ideas but had no way of getting capital to begin a business," said Hapsatou Bal, a project credit officer. "They had no collateral. They had nothing to give but their dignity."[6]

These factors—illiteracy; a sense of powerlessness and lack of community cohesiveness; and low incomes inadequate for people to meet basic needs—compelled World Vision to work with Arafat residents. Other common human needs later cited by the community included concerns in the areas of health, education and the environment.

THE PROJECT

The Road of Hope[7] Urban Project began in 1994 "to empower people to carry out their own development process . . . through the establishment of a network of community institutions that will serve as catalysts for the social and economic development of the community through trained (local) leadership."[8] The program was planned to last 10 years, including community organizing, literacy, micro-enterprise development, youth organizing and primary school education. Child sponsorship, in partnership with World Vision Germany, was introduced in December 1997 in both Arafat and another provincial town, Kiffa, in the Assaba Region. The main reason for introducing child sponsorship was to reorient programs to the special needs of children and to provide a longer-term source of funding beyond shorter partnerships that had characterized donor giving to World Vision Mauritania. Most foundations and large private donors gave for an average of three years. A heavy burden was imposed on program staff to do fundraising over and above the already heavy weight of development work. This stress on staff was multiplied during times of higher-level planning meetings when questions arose about whether the organization could afford to stay in Mauritania. On the other hand, child sponsors tend to give consistently from the time a child enters school until the child finishes high school. As long as they feel informed about the child's progress and receive information showing the positive impact their contributions are making, it is not difficult to satisfy donors' needs.

Of the project's 42 staff, all are Mauritanians except the original project director, a Dutch woman, and her successor, an Ethiopian. The project's micro-enterprise unit has given 103 loans averaging US$1,100 each; 55 percent of the unit's clients are women; its average repayment rate is 96 percent.

COMMUNITY ORGANIZING METHOD

What makes Mauritania different?

Four contextual factors set the stage for any discussion about community organization in the capital city of Mauritania.

Mauritania bridges Arab North Africa and south of the Sahara

This metaphor of a bridge, first expressed by the founding president of Mauritania, describes the country's sensitive geography along the divide between Arab/Berber and black African cultures. These two cultures have not shared a placid cohabitation. As early as the 10th century, Berber tribes chafed against the might of the Ghana empire, which coveted the Berber caravan city of Aoudaghost. Aoudaghost's ruins are in present-day Mauritania. The Ghana empire conquered and ruled the city for a short while during that same century. The austere Muslim Berbers (converted during the first forays of Arabs against the Berbers) then rose up in defiance against the Ghana empire and surrounding territories. They fought fiercely and regained their city in 1054, succeeding in eventually taking over for a brief time Koumbi Saleh, the famed capital city of the Ghana empire. These ruins are also visible in present-day Mauritania.

The Moors, descendants of the Arab/Berber Islamization begun in the 8th century and furthered in the 15th, firmly established Islam and Hassaniya Arabic in Mauritania by the 19th century. Skirmishes with surrounding black African kingdoms such as the Djoloff and the Tekrour continued well into the 1900s.[9] The present-day Woloff tribe, some of whom reside in Mauritania, are descendants of the ancient kingdom of Djoloff. Likewise, the Peulhs of today have their roots in the old kingdom of Tekrour.

The Moors hold the reins of power in modern Mauritania and have done so since independence from France in November 1960. While modern urban life is slowly changing their traditional way of living—so closely linked to the desert, the tent, and camels—they still retain their inscrutability, self-confidence and freedom from subservience to hierarchical authority. They sometimes live with a sense of bringing the village to the city and have a strong sense of mutual reciprocity in relationships. Arafat's Moors are its most numerous people group.

The Halpulaar are one with the proud nomads called the Peulh, who have ranged over the expansive spaces of West Africa with their cattle for centuries. In modern Mauritania many of their number are educated professionals. They traditionally lived along the fertile banks of the Senegal River but no longer roam as much over the sub-region with their cattle, many of which were decimated in past droughts. They still retain some elements of their traditional culture such as a deep sense of connection with their rural villages and great respect for elders and traditional leaders.

The Soninke are more numerous in Mali, but many reside in Mauritania. They are descendants of the once-powerful Ghana empire, and are esteemed by the Moors, who sometimes intermarry with them. They are industrious, disciplined in work habits and very attached to the extended family structure.

All three people groups can be found in the urban settlements of Nouakchott. Community organization has been more successful when approaching them as distinct groups. Community associations in Nouakchott tend also to be grouped along these ethnic lines. Among youth, however, less and less emphasis is placed on these distinctions, particularly among youth involved with Road of Hope Urban Project.

Mauritania is an Islamic republic

By the grace of God, the government has allowed World Vision, a Christian organization, to work in Mauritania since 1984. By and large, World Vision's work with partner communities is respected because the impact is visible and most of our staff are competent and respected Mauritanians. One can imagine that our Christian identity and personnel sometimes come under scrutiny. In some cases these elements are weighed against the perceived value of the development work we do. The scale, thus far, has tipped in favor of appreciating the development work accomplished.

Under Islamic law, all Mauritanians are considered to be Muslims. World Vision, as a guest in Mauritania, respects this provision in its daily interactions with staff in the workplace and in working with community members. Expatriate Christians, however, are not prohibited from praying and meeting for worship, and a Catholic church operating in Mauritania, established before independence, has various parishes in different parts of the country. There is also no prohibition in Islam on respectful discussions about faith between expatriate Christians and nationals. These are only possible, however, in an atmosphere of friendship, sincere love and true respect for each other as human beings created by God.

Naturally, classic Christian community organization theory and practice, in which churches are an essential partner in the community, simply can't work in Mauritania.

Mauritania experienced civilian rule, then military, then civilian

For the first 24 years after independence, Mauritania was ruled by a civilian government led by Mokhtar Ould Daddah. He introduced Arabic as the national language, aligned his country closer with Arab North Africa and focused on development of the capital city to the detriment of rural areas. The first coup installing a military government took place in July 1978, followed by three successive coups within one year. Finally, in 1980, Colonel M. Khouna Haidallah took power and stayed at the helm of the country for four years. In 1984, while attending a summit meeting in Bujumbura, Burundi, he was overthrown by Colonel Maaouya Ould Sid Ahmed Taya, a seasoned yet discreet man who has ruled Mauritania firmly since that time. President Taya eventually introduced municipal elections in the late 1980s and then won the first presidential election in 1992. He was reelected president in 1997.

Many people who hold real power in the country are closely linked to the military regime that ruled the country for many years. Because of this, mediation—defined by Robert Linthicum as an "effort to get the governmental or economic powers of the city to understand what they are obligated by law to provide but are not providing"[10]—must be approached carefully, wisely and gently. Demonstrations and marches are unlikely to produce a positive outcome in a place known to crack down hard on such incidents. The notion of rights being obligated by law also assumes a widely accepted notion of the rule of law—a notion rarely entrenched in the young democracies of Africa. Furthermore, any linkage of such actions to the development organization, a foreign NGO, would be quickly interpreted in a manner detrimental to the good relationships forged with local and national leadership.

Nouakchott is a young city inhabited by traditionally nomadic people

A foreign organization intending to work in Nouakchott needs to understand this fact, particularly as it relates to community organization. Many problems encountered in larger and older cities of the world, and the classic community organization techniques developed and nurtured to address these problems, do not apply to Nouakchott. There is no fleeing of the inner city for the suburbs, no grabbing of prime land by the greedy rich, no industries polluting where the poor live and exploiting their labor, no organized youth gangs terrorizing residents, no volunteers available to assist their neighborhoods.

Learning by doing

When the first project expatriate staff moved into Arafat in 1994 to begin systematically visiting people and building bridges, they decided to live in the community. All the staff rented rooms in the community and participated in the community's daily life. A key learning from this experience was that staff, rather than the community, benefited most from the living arrangement. Results included greater empathy, and greater understanding of and identification with the community's struggles and victories. At least two hours a day were devoted to prayer during the first year. God was faithful in preparing the way for work in Arafat through this persistent and faithful praying by expatriate staff. We believe that the success of the Road of Hope Urban Project today in Arafat is due to the foundation of prayer established from that time.

From the beginning the mayor of Arafat was a strong supporter of the project. His support opened the way for project staff into Arafat, and his support nurtured community-development activities.

After coalitions organized around specific areas of interest in 1994, the greatest enthusiasm was expressed toward small-business development and credit. Five groups became the first recipients of loans for micro-enterprises. After the first formal evaluation, we learned that full reimbursement of loans did not mean the project was succeeding. Some clients paid back loans in full, yet ended up just as poor as before. To overcome this, a rigorous system of assessing clients' business plans before granting loans focused on determining viability of the business to operate at a level where the profits could repay the loan *and* provide increased income to the client. One unfortunate outcome of this more rigorous screening was that the poorest stood less and less chance of getting loans, since their businesses were rarely ongoing concerns. To date, the project has not identified a lasting solution to this issue. A system of evaluating clients' quality of life during and after repayment of the loan attempted to ensure that project staff quickly noticed if the weight of repayment was taking too high a toll and remedial measures such as rescheduling the loan could be taken. Success in practically utilizing the information being collected remains minimal. One measure of relief for clients, implemented after a second major evaluation of the micro-enterprise project, was to lower the "administrative fee" (the term used in order to avoid offending Islamic values, which forbid the charging of interest).

Another very important lesson was that community organizing by expatriate staff did not work well at all. There were too many layers of culture between expatriates and the community to peel off within established time frames. Further, trust developed a few people at a time and only after a large investment of time. In the case of getting literacy activities off the ground, it took nine months of false starts and reluctance to collaborate by the government ministry charged with adult literacy until the project hired Ahmed Ould Abdellahi, who used to work with the same ministry. He knew his way through the system and could get things done. He had the trust and confidence of those in authority, particularly for a well-guarded domain like adult literacy, where literacy primers can be used to teach virtually anything to the populace. One story illustrates this well: Someone reported falsely to a senior government official that World Vision was teaching Christianity to Mauritanians through its adult literacy activities. The official asked which Mauritanians were present and was told, "Ahmed Ould Abdellahi is there." The official replied, "If Ahmed is there, then let them continue teaching it because it must be a good thing." The presence of competent and respected Mauritanian colleagues did more to advance the work than any expatriate could have.

A further lesson learned in Arafat was that community organizing gained credibility *after* and not before the start of community-development activities. This is contrary to a 1994 evaluation of four key urban development projects in different countries of the world. That finding concluded, "The evaluations demonstrate that community organizing provides an essential base upon which economic development, health care, education, housing projects and truly holistic development can occur."[11] By the time community organizing began in Arafat in 1996, community development activities in micro-enterprise, literacy and youth work were well developed. Arafat residents, community leaders and national leaders had developed respect and appreciation for the project's work. Clearly, in the case of Arafat, it was essential to start activities identified through Participatory Rural Appraisal techniques and participant observation methods. The growth and success of these early activities developed a credibility base from which community organizing was relaunched. By this time, a competent Mauritanian named Abeidy Ould Brahalla, with long experience as a trainer with the Peace Corps, was available to lead the community-organizing process onward.

Currently, Road of Hope Urban Project staff are not certain what their role should be, if any, in sensitizing leadership to the issue of resettling "squatters" on allocated land. The project has been reluctant to invest heavily in development activities in the *gazra* because of uncertain investment durability, particularly for infrastructure such as schools and water. Only recently has acceptance grown that *gazra* dwellers might remain for a long time and should not be denied opportunities equivalent to those living in allocated land.

EMERGING EXAMPLES OF TRANSFORMATIONAL RESULTS AND IMPACTS

Community organizing has given new hope and costs less money

Linking community associations with other institutions that can provide assistance means the community does not become dependent on the development organization. Additionally, getting people to do for themselves whatever is best for them builds confidence and positive community energy. A story illustrating this point started in the mayor's office and involved one man, his school, the project director and a flag:

Elbou Ould Isselmou met Renny De Kleine, the project director, at the mayor's office, where he had gone to ask for a flag for their primary school. He was the president of the parent/teacher association, which had done a remarkable job of mobilizing the community to start a school. The community had pieced together some wooden shacks to serve as classrooms but had no money left for furniture. As he talked with De Kleine about the association's dream of a better school, De Kleine became convinced her team had a role to play in enabling the community to achieve this dream. Shortly thereafter, project staff trained association members to write a project proposal for the furniture. Staff also encouraged them to approach the local government with a request to build a better school building in their community. Although the government's particular program covered construction of rural schools only, the association convinced them to underwrite construction of their school. At *the same time they produced and submitted to the U.S. embassy their proposal for furniture. Both requests were granted by the end of 1996, and construction of the school was started and completed the following year. The completed school building is valued at US$35,000, while the furniture bought with the U.S. embassy grant cost US$6,000. Project investment included the cost of training meetings for the association and the availability of its community organizers.*

Youth organizing—the unexpected success

When youth organizing started in 1994, it was not seen by some staff as a serious activity that merited attention. After all, what did providing soccer balls and organizing drama, dance and other cultural activities have to do with transformational development in the midst of poverty? Ahmed El Hor, the youth coordinator, and his team labored on. They strengthened youth associations, developed links among them, organized televised sports events such as soccer tournaments and cross-country races that even included some girls, and trained youth to produce quality theater productions that people paid to see. Skepticism began to turn to surprise. The youth started an Arafat-wide newspaper that contained local news and humor aimed at those who merited it, and information about better health practices such as how to stop smoking, prevent AIDS and maintain better hygiene. The project contributed some reams of photocopying paper. The youth also started an Arafat-wide radio service broadcasting similar information. They saved the money and bought the equipment themselves. Soon a youth center opened, with project help. Youth now use the center to teach skills such as T-shirt printing, painting and typewriting. From there, they organize theater for Arafat residents, and movie nights on development themes.

Two major sports activities organized each year are sometimes broadcast on national television if an important dignitary attends. These include a cross-country run for young boys and one for older boys and girls. The fact that girls are even involved in such activities is a testimony to how much transformation has taken place with respect to cultural traditions that forbid girls to dress in sports clothes that display their legs. The other sport is an annual soccer tournament. These and other events cited provide tremendous opportunities to teach valuable lessons on morality, respect, tolerance for each other and working together. Youth have described their mission in their own words, "We want to plant equality and justice between the members of our society. We want to develop our cultural skills. We want to create a generation that will face the new world. We want to develop the youth and a responsible nation, that the world might be a world of communion between all people and between all members of society." Other statements by these youth show the level of transformation in their lives, as heard during an evaluation conducted by Ken Luscombe and Laura Benson in August 1997:

- "Through our newspaper, we want to make an impact in the community. We are trying to change the bad things in our community: crime, drugs, AIDS, social sickness."
- "If we are succeeding in our work, it is due to the youth program that has enabled us to help our community. You can see here in Arafat some associations know what they are doing; they are real."
- "The after-school activities have helped me to do better in my school work. We were not really studying at the school, but when we began doing after-school activities it encouraged us to study."
- In response to a question about who "owns" activities: "We do. World Vision could not do this work without us. We could do our work without World Vision, but it would not be the same quality. But after a time it will be the same quality and even better."

Clearly, a foundation for more permanent and lasting change is being built among youth.

The blind see, the deaf hear and lives are saved

As a metaphor for what adult literacy has accomplished in Arafat, people use such words. Literacy is a skill which, once acquired, is lasting and indisputably evident. The pleasure and joy of learning to read, write and calculate for the first time in one's adult life can only be described by those who have done it. In 1998, 92 percent of the students were women. The following represent some results of literacy training:

- Parents with school-age children state that they can now follow their children's homework and read written information from the school.
- Students learn from their literacy booklets how germs are passed, the importance of washing hands before eating or preparing food, the importance of home cleanliness and how to disinfect water with a few drops of bleach.
- Students better appreciate the damaging consequences of divorce, which in Arafat has left 38 percent of households headed by single mothers. Students learn things they can do to nurture a more wholesome family life.
- Women express greater confidence in themselves as they move from feeling uneducated to feeling educated.
- Students sense better integration into the modern life of the city (being literate was not formerly necessary in daily nomadic life). Now, they can read road signs and billboards, read newspapers and make telephone calls from public phone booths.
- Students are more effective members of business cooperatives. They can calculate profit margins, write lists of raw material to be bought and keep records of goods sold.

- Mothers can now read instructions on how to dispense prescribed medicine to their sick children. Mariam Saleck, a mother who lives in Arafat, took her sick daughter Fatima to a local clinic, which also has a pharmacy. She was given medicine for her daughter's sickness with written and oral instructions for its use. While there, she asked the pharmacist for medicine for her goat, also sick. (It is not uncommon for pharmacies in Mauritania to also sell veterinary products.) The pharmacist gave her some tablets for her goat, with written instructions on how to use the medicine. Mariam went home, and when it was time to administer the medicine, gave her daughter the pills for the goat and the goat her daughter's medicine. The results were nearly fatal for the little girl. Mariam could have read the instructions if she were literate. The experience prompted her to join the literacy classes offered by Road of Hope Urban Project.

Group power, bridge-building, sharing, and a bright picture of the future strengthen a sense of community

Other emerging elements of transformation include a newfound sense of collaboration among Arafat's residents and a broadening circle of partnerships. Sharing benefits of development among community members is always an indicator of emerging transformation. So is having a positive and bright picture of the future of one's community.

The president of the parent/teacher association said, "We have learned a lot over the past year. We have gained confidence in ourselves and in the group. There is strong community support, and we are developing friendships with each other and partnerships with other organizations. We keep the government informed. They support and appreciate our efforts." He went on to add, "We are both a school and a development association. We want to change the water problem by getting a school connection to the main line, and a community connection so that we can sell water in the area. We want people to benefit from the placement of the water pipe. There are many benefits for the community that can come with the availability of water. Gardens and trees can be planted to increase the quality of life, and money can be generated from the sale of water to fund other projects. We will buy a hose pipe to serve the families around the school, which will save them money and help improve their quality of life."

TENTATIVE CONCLUSIONS ABOUT TRANSFORMATION IN ARAFAT

Road of Hope Urban Project is in its fifth year, which is not a long time with reference to change and transformation in a community like Arafat. Some tentative conclusions can be drawn from what has been described in the preceding pages. There is nothing extraordinary about what has happened, except to those who have lived the experience. Road of Hope Urban Project staff find it extraordinary that the community trusts them and wants to collaborate. The community finds it extraordinary that these staff members work with them in a manner that is helping them improve their lives. The government finds it extraordinary that Road of Hope Urban Project has achieved so much and yet gives credit to the community. So, what can be affirmed about the transformational development framework adopted by the Road of Hope Urban Program in Arafat?

Success is expatriate Christian staff and Mauritanian Muslim staff working well together. Strengths and capacities that each bring to the program have been complementary. Some things could be done well only by one and not another and vice versa. The ability to work well together has become a cherished value for all staff, despite daily challenges to this value.

Presence is of paramount importance. A number of national staff live in Arafat today. Their work has become their community life. They spend weekends and holidays meeting residents over numerous cups of sweet mint tea. They influence opinions, change perspectives and show appreciation in a culture in which the volume of communication is the barometer of relationships.

Fervent, persistent prayer to God is the foundation for transformation. Some still sneer, as in the early days when project staff spent a lot of time praying. At that time critics suggested that there were few activities to show for all the praying. But work in Mauritania demands great patience and persistent prayer. Fruit may come many years later, but it will certainly come. No work of enduring quality can be established in Mauritania without the prayers of men and women whose hearts burn to see transformation in the lives of human beings. May God give to Mauritania more people like this.

Methodology should be shaped by action-reflection-action. Road of Hope Urban Project staff learned not to follow slavishly community organization orthodoxy. Staff tested methods first, thought about what to adapt, then applied appropriate action. This experimental mindset emphasized the goal of seeking what worked best for their context.

Visible impact speaks louder than words when it comes to alleviating poverty. The government has often said to project staff that what impresses them is the project's concrete results. Studies and research definitely have their place in any development project; however, they must never take the place of actions that have a high chance of success and that foster trust among the organization, the community and other partners.

Challenges remain. Micro-enterprise clients complained often during the 1997 evaluation about the administrative fee charged. What about the poorest, who can't even run a business with capacity to repay the loans? The project must continue to struggle for a solution to this issue in its development framework. Also, lessons learned while monitoring changes in quality of life for current clients must be documented and used to improve the way the development organization promotes transformation of the poor who borrow from the organization. Additionally, Road of Hope Urban Project must examine the efficiency of the micro-enterprise project. The struggle now is to make it competitive yet still service oriented. It must operate like any successful business, yet retain regular contact with clients that goes beyond a mere business relationship.

A FEW WORDS ABOUT TRANSFORMATIONAL WORK AS A REFLECTION OF WITNESS

Expatriate Christian staff members in World Vision Mauritania find daily opportunities to witness through the quality of their work, the quality of their prayer, the quality of their relationships and the quality of what they say they believe about God. When people credit us with good work, we in turn give glory to God in their hearing, whenever possible. We share our requests and answers to prayer, as opportunity comes. When crises occur, we openly share how we trust in God to deliver us. When God does deliver, we ascribe it to God's care. We pray for those who don't mind our doing so, and we discuss Christianity and Islam with those who want to do so. We never pressure anyone to change religions. We strive to ensure consistency between how we live and what the Bible teaches about sound Christian conduct. Often our Muslim colleagues challenge us to live consistently with our beliefs. They watch us closely for examples of consistency. Our greatest testimony, we find, is to love people unconditionally. Sincere love is recognized, but hypocrisy quickly becomes a subject of scorn. We are always ready to answer questions to which the gospel is the answer, and we let God do the rest.

Notes

[1] *It-tahaddur Journal* (1980). Reference taken from the Road of Hope Urban Project Planning document.

[2] Mauritanian City Census (1977) and UN (1974). Reference taken from the Road of Hope Urban Project Planning document.

[3] *New York Times* (March 1985). Reference taken from the Road of Hope Urban Project Planning document.

[4] Nouakchott's water, of excellent quality, comes from 67 kilometers east of the city, where the water is pumped up from deep aquifers under the desert sand.

[5] L. Benson and K. Luscombe, "Fostering Leadership in Nouakchott" (*Together*, October–December 1997), 12–16.

[6] Karen Homer, "A Loan to Dye for," *World Vision (USA) Magazine* (December 1997/January 1998), 9–11.

[7] Road of Hope is the actual name of a road running east from Nouakchott across the lower third of Mauritania. It is the only road that cuts across that part of the Sahara Desert.

[8] Road of Hope Urban Project Planning Document (1994–98), 11.

[9] Catherine Belvaude, *La Mauritanie* (Paris: Karthala, 1989).

[10] Robert Linthicum, "Working with the Urban Poor," *Together* (October–December 1994), 15.

[11] Ibid., 3.

PART FOUR

FRONTIERS

7

The Contribution
of Community Development
to Peace-building

SIOBHAN O'REILLY

The aim of this report is to investigate the contribution that Area Development Programs (ADPs) can bring to peace-building, most notably in reducing the potential for and the effect of violent "identity" conflicts. In so doing, it hopes to identify key elements within the ADP approach that have a capacity to encourage peace-building, whether in the prevention, management or reconciliation of such conflict. Consequently, we hope to strengthen awareness and understanding of how community development can and does contribute to the building of peace in the developing world both for our benefit and that of the wider NGO community.

OVERVIEW

Rationale

The motivation for this research came from multiple sources. Chiefly it emerged in response to the crisis in confidence that humanitarian interna-

This chapter is condensed from a report published in the UK in April 1999. For brevity's sake, comprehensive sections on methodology, theoretical foundations, and presentations of the research itself are not included. Rather, an overview of findings so far is presented in hopes of encouraging dialogue and further inquiry. For more depth and detail, please refer to the full report, available through World Vision United Kingdom, Policy and Research Department, or order through the Web at www.worldvision.org.uk.

tional nongovernmental organizations (INGOs) have been undergoing in the 1990s as they struggle to respond to the increasingly demanding and complex impacts of modern intra-state war.

Such a climate has provided healthy challenges to INGOs. Serious questioning is emerging in relation to the efficacy of aid, the manner in which it is offered, and how it needs to be integrated into a more comprehensive response that advocates a political resolution of conflicts. Additionally, many INGOs that also engage in long-term development are questioning how they can promote the prevention or resolution of such conflict and the process of reconciliation among divided societies. In so doing, an array of initiatives and programs have been adopted both by INGOs and conflict consultancy NGOs that seek to better equip them to respond appropriately and professionally to such challenging circumstances.

Such a response has not been without its fair share of criticism, the most common being that INGOs are not sufficiently equipped or accountable to engage in such work. In addition, peace-building has become "ghettoized," put in a box, conscribed to workshops or specific programs to be implemented alongside other rehabilitation or development programs.

Yet what has been overlooked in the rush to deal with the problem at hand is the inherent peace-building capacity that already exists within current development methodology. It is common knowledge that development practice has the capacity to build social capital, networks of trust, cooperation and organization. Yet this has not been translated into research into what generic community-development methodology has to offer in this regard and how it can be strengthened and consciously used as a peace-building tool. Although it is recognized that factors behind violent intra-state wars are often macro-political and economic, many of them rely on grassroots support and even participation for their momentum.

Why ADPs?

Area Development Programs are a specific type of integrated rural community-development program that has become the principal channel through which we seek to assist the poor throughout the world. Currently, there are some 238 ADPs in 35 countries around the world, with more being added each year.

Anecdotal evidence indicated that Area Development Programs held peace-building potential. ADPs are sustainable, integrated community-development programs that cover an area the size of an administrative district. Despite their size they are implemented at the micro-level (village) and rely on a network of committees formed of elected community members to oversee the running of the programs at various levels throughout the district.

Owing to their geographical size and the fact that they rely on the principle of interaction and cooperation among all beneficiaries, they cause a large number of people groups with different religious, ethnic and political identities to work together toward one aim, that is, community development.

Methodology and approach

The research investigated two dimensions: field study and literature review. The former involved visiting five ADPs, two in Asia (Orissa State, India; and Cox's Bazaar, Bangladesh) for the pilot research and three in Africa (Masaka District, Uganda; southeast Ethiopia; and Kwahu District, Ghana) for the final research, in order to examine the actual and potential peace-building impact of current ADPs. The literature review was conducted in order to provide a theoretical foundation for the research: theories of conflict, causes of modern conflict, civil society, reconciliation and peace-building.

Methodology for the field research had to be developed during a pilot study. The fact that no base-line indicators existed also meant that different methods had to be tried out, including tests to see if it was possible to obtain community-based indicators. Primarily, Participatory Rural Appraisal techniques were used, and control groups were also studied in order to compare the findings with communities beyond the ADP. Because the methodology proved to be largely appropriate and was changed little, and because the ADPs in Asia were found to have some strikingly different characteristics, the pertinent findings of the pilot research have been included in the analysis.

The indicators used to measure the peace-building capacity were based on the hypothesis that ADPs contribute to peace-building by encouraging increased, meaningful interaction, cooperation and interdependence among all people groups.

Summary of findings

The insight gained from the research has been illuminating, encouraging and challenging for the fields of peace-building, community development and natural resource management.

Peace-building and good development practice

First of all, it is clear that peace-building and transformational community development are intimately linked. There appears to be a direct connection between effective, participatory grassroots development and peace-building. A dual lesson is to be learned; peace-building should not be seen as an irrelevant activity that is a distraction from the business of poverty reduction.

Capacity to create a peace-building environment

ADPs clearly have a strong capacity to generate a culture of mutual understanding, interdependence and trust among diverse people groups. This

114   SIOBHAN O'REILLY

emerges as an indirect result of the development process, the approach used and the structure around which the ADP operates. The participatory, all-embracing approach in which all beneficiaries are encouraged to work together toward one aim, the structure of committee networks that connect communities throughout the ADP, and the role of an independent coordinating agent all combine to create a powerful peace-building environment.

By peace-building environment we mean an environment in which conflicting parties can become reconciled, disputes are more easily resolved or managed peacefully, and the likelihood of violent conflict is reduced. The latter refers to the increased interdependence and building of solidarity between diverse ethnic or religious groups and their leaders that the ADP brings about. This, in turn, reduces the leverage for manipulation of prejudices or differences by conflict entrepreneurs, who frequently exploit such differences. It also builds local capacities for peace should war break out.

General outcomes found in the ADPs researched were the erosion of ethnic and sectarian prejudice, mistrust and division; transformation of inter-community dynamics; reconciliation of conflicting parties; the growth of deep respect for human dignity; and a certain measure of ADP-wide solidarity.

Catalysts

Certain peace-building catalysts have been identified. These are the formation of heterogeneous, voluntary development committees that are representative of all the different communities and which are connected from the village to district level; the all-embracing approach of the development agency; the role and example of village development workers or facilitators; the strengthening of local churches; racially mixed education; and the role of community celebration.

Capacity varies and depends on structure, approach and process

The existence of these catalysts in each ADP depends on the exact structure, approach and process used. However, because ADPs are not homogeneous and details of design vary from region to region, the degree to which they encourage peace-building is variable.

Lessons for natural resource management

One area of peace-building in which ADPs are demonstrating excellent competence and which needs little extra attention is local dispute management. By building the capacity of local leaders and, above all, by causing them to become familiar with one another, the ability to resolve local disputes has markedly improved. This has important lessons for natural resource management.

Potential greater than reality—the need for a peace-building perspective

However, in spite of the above, it must be stressed that the peace-building capacity of many ADPs so far lies more in their potential than their actual performance—the full extent of their capacity remains untapped. This is because their peace-building capacity has neither been recognized by ADP managers nor consciously been managed toward that aim. Therefore, for the peace-building capacity of ADPs to be substantial or influential they require specific and careful management toward this aim. Peace-building using the ADP model requires few extra financial resources; what is required is a peace-building perspective.

Second, there is an important aspect of the ADP model not being fully employed or taken advantage of, one that has enormous potential not only for peace-building but also for community development. This is the opportunity for coalitions and forums at the level beyond the village or parish, which provide an excellent platform for economics of scale and collective advocacy on issues of common concern.

Eight points for peace-building

In order to exploit fully the peace-building potential of ADPs, and indeed many other community-development programs, certain key insights and lessons need to be applied. Most of these involve merely applying a peace-building perspective to the design and management of ADPs, but there are also some specific concrete measures that need to be taken:

1. The more participatory, the more peace-building.
2. Slow, gradual entry with emphasis on relationship building.
3. Influence of the agent of change: the need for impartiality.
4. Formation of committees—representative, voluntary and district-wide.
5. Coalitions and apex groups—tapping into the potential to "think ADP."
6. Training and education in civil society for the beneficiaries.
7. The need to integrate the non-poor into the process.
8. Regionalization of ADPs to be considered.

Limitation of ADPs

It is important to note the many limitations of ADPs in peace-building. ADPs cannot hope to influence the full range of types of conflict or the complex factors that affect them. We recognize that they can only make a *contribution*.

ADPs rarely influence top-level actors: macro factors such as the political economy or historical formation of the state, predatory leaders or political associations, globalization or global systemic poverty. The crucial importance of targeting these contributors to modern conflict, where possible, is increasingly being recognized. This is not, however, an area that ADPs can influence unless the concept of regionalization of ADPs is considered.

Second, as long as ADPs do not integrate the local rich or non-poor into the process, they do not have the ability to restore full dignity to the poor and to defray latent conflict inherent within unjust economic relationships. If we are to apply the holistic understanding of peace-building as defined in this report, ADPs would not match up.

Areas for consideration

Due consideration must be given to the fact that this research is relatively preliminary—the ADP sample was modest, and the ADP concept is comparatively young. The true test for this research has to be time. One can never prove the success of a program in conflict prevention until the region undergoes a serious threat to peace. However, it is clear that strong potential exists within this approach. The challenge is to incorporate a more deliberate approach to the implementation of ADPs, and community development, that exploits the inherent peace-building capacity to its fullest potential.

This requires facing another challenge and is neatly summarized in the following quote: "The true challenge is to integrate a sensitivity to conflict into the vision of development" (World Bank 1998).

BACKGROUND

Geopolitical changes and the "new world disorder"

Since 1990 the toll of intra-state conflict has been immense: over 4 million people killed, 24 million internally displaced and 18 million more refugees.[1]

Contrary to common belief, the post–Cold War period has not witnessed a dramatic increase in numbers of wars.[2] What *has* changed, however, is the type and nature of these conflicts: conflicts are typically intra-state and characterized by guerrilla warfare, separatist movements and ethnic violence over issues of governance and territory, and are primarily manifested as "identity conflicts," as classified by E. Regehr.[3] A particularly distinct characteristic is that noncombatants are the main victims—around 90 percent of victims are civilians as compared with 15 percent in World War I.[4] This is because civilians are commonly the target of control by the main players and used as weapons in conflicts that rely on the manipulation of ethnic ideology more than defending geographical front lines.

Yet although these wars are "internal" by definition, their impact is often international; neighboring populations are drawn in and refugees flood across borders, often spreading into Europe and the Americas.[5] As a consequence, the international community is increasingly being expected to use its diplomatic and military prowess to resolve crises that threaten regional stability, drain UN resources and are morally repugnant to a world audience that is fed a daily diet of crisis news by the media and the Internet.

The demise of the Cold War effectively lifted the lid on long-running, latent-yet-contained conflicts in Africa and Eastern Europe and unleashed a frenzy of violence and social breakdown that the global community was ill-prepared for. The highly sophisticated arms networks and training of governments in warfare rather than governance left the soil ripe for continued, less disciplined warfare.[6] The fundamental impact of globalization has also been identified as culpable in creating and maintaining the momentum for wars that are waged over control of resources.[7]

The problem of conflict and the birth of the new "conflict orthodoxy"

The effect this has had on nongovernmental organizations, governmental and UN agencies, diplomats and politicians has been pervasive and wholesale. Humanitarian agencies have found their activities and resources increasingly consumed as they respond to the impact of violent conflict, while the fruit of years of development work has been destroyed as communities are physically and emotionally uprooted.

The new political landscape has also meant that engagement by the international community in preventing or resolving conflicts is hesitant, incoherent and piecemeal, often resulting in failure, for example, UNISOM in Somalia. With the replacement of bipolar geopolitical ideology with the crusade for neo-liberal free markets, Western powers have become less inclined to participate in foreign conflicts. Furthermore, the complexity of these crises that are multi-actor, regional, and involve non-state actors has rendered conventional diplomatic and analytical skills inappropriate. As a result, the international community has tended to be complacent, ill-equipped or reticent in responding to these crises. Instead, humanitarian aid is offered as a moral palliative, causing humanitarian NGOs to "become front-line troops for governments which prefer humanitarian help to political solutions" (World Disasters Report, 1997). Such exposure has led to criticism from media, politicians and NGO practitioners and theorists as international humanitarian NGOs (INGOs) have attempted to fill the gap.[8] Criticism also arose from the realization that what were now outdated approaches were feeding the warring parties as much as the victims.[9]

The need to pursue alternative forms of diplomacy from those based on the traditional ideological paradigms has pushed INGOs and NGOs into further prominence in the area of conflict resolution and into greater areas of partnership with governmental organizations. Indeed, the need for multi-track and preventive diplomacy has begun to be recognized by the UN,

European Union and national governments on account of their own inability to conduct unofficial networking and mediation away from the glare of media lights.[10] This has brought about a quiet revolution in accepting the valid and effective role of the church and religious individuals in mediation work.[11]

Impact on humanitarian NGOs—the new peace agenda

Within the humanitarian industry the impact has been equally challenging. As the new environment has challenged their very credibility and effectiveness, INGOs have been forced to do much soul-searching over what their role should be. For many, the experience has shaken corporate self-confidence in the ability to provide humane, beneficial assistance in an increasingly complex world. But for some it has also led to much needed review and reform. First, current emergency programs have been examined for ways in which they might prevent exacerbating conflict or at least "do no harm."[12] Second, many INGOs and NGOs have sought to expand their role to include engagement in specific conflict resolution, reconciliation and peace-building programs. And third, early warning and advocacy aimed at achieving conflict prevention and resolution at macro-political levels have been aggressively pursued.[13] Many NGOs attempt to further integrate emergency and rehabilitation approaches with those of community-development programs in recognition of the cyclical nature of these crises.

The second development has led to a range of initiatives that aim to promote the prevention or resolution of violent conflict and the process of reconciliation among divided societies. These include democratization, demobilization of soldiers, strengthening of civil society, developing respect for human rights, psychosocial trauma workshops for victims, and training of staff in grassroots conflict management. Examples include the following:

- Oxfam Sudan requested Responding to Conflict, a UK-based training NGO, to conduct a workshop for its staff in Khartoum in 1996 to help them in analyzing and identifying their role in conflict and how they might design their program accordingly.
- World Vision Sudan, Germany, Senegal and Rwanda have hosted a number of Local Capacity for Peace workshops to sensitize and equip NGO staff from the regions in the negative impact of aid delivery to conflict contexts and the use of indigenous communities' capacity to build peace.
- ACORD is running a program aimed at strengthening local capacities for building peace in Uganda by expanding and strengthening the role of traditional chiefs in conflict management.
- ActionAid has gained a reputation for its innovative projects in Burundi and Somaliland, the former using the simple game of football as a means of encouraging interaction and teamwork among unemployed

young men. Formation of colline communities, which included young people, were set up to discuss and facilitate community needs. Football matches were also used as a part of the effort to create friendly interaction between Hutus and Tutsis.

- African Evangelical Enterprise facilitates religious-based reconciliation workshops for church leaders in Rwanda.
- World Vision's work with ex-child soldiers and traumatized children, notably the Traumatized Children's Program in Gulu, north Uganda, and the Creative Activities for Trauma Healing (CATH) schools project in Bosnia.
- Oxfam has launched a major three-year public campaign in the UK, Cut Conflict, to seek governmental policy change in four areas: to curb the arms trade; to bring war criminals to justice; to promote peace through general aid, trade and economic policies; and to uphold the rights of refugees. This is a high-profile public campaign that brings the issue of conflict and its centrality to development issues to the domain of its members.
- Oxfam is also promoting the idea of Conflict Impact Assessments to be adopted by governments, companies and NGOs in order to assess the risk of aid, trade or policies to unstable countries around the world.
- World Vision Bosnia's micro-enterprise programs are designed to increase economic relations among Muslim, Croat and Serb groups and also to restore and develop civil society. The programs have attracted attention from the World Bank for their innovative, sensitive and effective approach to peace-building.
- The Catholic Institute for International Relations (CIIR) is running a three year advocacy and research project on the role of civil organizations in peace and democratization processes in Colombia, Guatemala, South Africa, Angola and East Timor.
- The UK Working Group on Landmines (UKWGLM) is a coalition of 50 UK-based NGOs set up to lobby for the global ban on anti-personnel landmines by the world's governments. It supports the work of the International Coalition. As such, it represents the move on the part of NGOs to lessen the impact of armed conflict on civilians.

This move into previously uncharted territory is not merely a reaction to the new working environment, nor is it merely "jumping on the bandwagon," as some have described it. (At least, for some it is not.) Rather, many INGOs and NGOs see reconciliation and peace-building work as something closely rooted to their vision and mission—a natural outworking of their community-development work that encourages social empowerment and change in peacetime, and interdependence and cooperation in the wake of violent conflict.[14] Nonviolent conflict, as a phenomenon of social change, is therefore accepted as a natural progression of effective development,[15] which is destabilizing by nature.[16] It is violent conflict that stands as the antithesis to what we work for[17] and that drives so many NGOs and INGOs to prevention, resolution or reconciliation.

Secular-based INGOs recognize the phenomenon of violent conflict as a central reality in the lives of the poor among whom they are working. Therefore it fits in with their mission of strengthening the capacity of the poor to deal with forces that impoverish them. Indeed, one INGO report states, "As a development agency it is our task to ensure that our understanding of conflict is built into our program design and that poor people are given increased capacity to prevent or deal with conflict related crises."[18] Meanwhile, Christian or faith-based organizations will also point to the fact that the concept of reconciliation lies at the heart of the gospel, which itself centers on restored relationships.

Lastly, the affiliation and proximity of development organizations to grassroots organizations, the ability to network and their nongovernmental status, are all attributes that indicate INGOs are well placed to make a contribution.[19]

In summary, agencies are attempting to "institutionalize reconciliation[20] and to integrate a wider sensitivity to conflict among its programs and staff.

Criticisms of the new peace agenda—the "ghettoizing" of peace-building and the need for mainstreaming

This adoption of the peace approach by INGOs has received its fair share of criticism from internal and external sources. Those who recognize the roots of conflict to be predominantly structural (macro-economic or political in nature) have criticized INGOs for focusing too heavily on developing what has come to be defined as "local capacities for peace" and for attempting to strengthen civil society in the absence of viable states.[21] An oft-cited criticism is that INGOs too often design their responses without a thorough analysis of conflict, a case of "practice preceding theory," which Voutira blames as the explanation for some INGO interventions worsening conflicts.[22] Constructive criticism from A. Carl gently warns against romanticizing the Local Capacities for Peace approach.[23] Many INGOs have themselves asked serious questions about whether or not outsiders can contribute.[24] For example, World Vision Bosnia has expressed great reservation on any initiatives that are not localized and fully integrated into the local context.[25]

The most common complaint is that little or no evaluation has been done to prove the effectiveness of humanitarian or peace NGOs in this field, particularly in the light of the hyperbole that surrounds it. Indeed, the relative lack of accountability and the fact that it has become fashionable to be seen to be "doing conflict work" warrants careful examination of impact. As a result, several major projects set up in the UK and funded by the Department for International Development attempt to set out common points of departure, definitions, conceptual frameworks and methods of analyzing impact.[26]

Such a reaction is not surprising—like a new pair of shoes, new paradigms usually seem unnecessary at first, are uncomfortable and have yet to be tested for their effectiveness.

Yet the critics have a point. Whether one agrees that peace-building is part of our mandate or capability, the fact is that INGOs are overlooking the role that *is* their comparative advantage—long-term community development. The majority of the debate and work tends to focus either on the response and influence of humanitarian agencies immediately before, during or after CHEs (complex humanitarian emergencies), or on specific peace-building programs to be implemented alongside other community-development or rehabilitation programs (with the exception of ActionAid). Some work has been done on the design of community-development projects to minimize the risk of natural resource-based disputes, but nothing has been done that the author is aware of on improvements in the design of community-development projects toward minimizing the risk of violent, ethnopolitical identity conflicts. [27] Yet this is an area that has been identified by others as necessary.[28]

What has been neglected is the study of the inherent peace-building[29] capacity that already exists within current development methodology. Examination of the contribution of generic processes, techniques and approaches that have been used for years in community development has attracted little attention in the peace-building drive, despite the fact that this would appear to be an obvious place to start. K. Bush identifies this tendency to neglect investigating the constructive impact of development projects as "ghettoizing" peace-building work, stating that the greatest peace-building impact will come from "these mainstream activities."[30] Aside from the fact that this is probably our strongest area of expertise, it has been overlooked largely due to the rush to deal with the problem at hand—emergencies—or to turn to the peace "experts."

Oddly enough, the place of social and economic community programs in building renewed trust, developing the dynamics of partnership and creating a stake for future cooperation is recognized in much of the literature on the subject.[31] Yet few people have translated this into practical research or programming. One reason, of course, is that the perspective is stuck at the level of looking at what can be done in the CHE response, not community development, and coming at it from the angle of specialists in peace and security studies and mediation. The fact that peace-related funding tends to be ad hoc and focused on immediate concerns further explains this tendency.[32]

Criticizing the approach taken by NGOs and INGOs to date is not the subject of this report. On the contrary, the author recognizes that this reflects the legitimate and necessary attempt of the international aid community to tackle the issue of conflict with a multidimensional, multi-sectoral approach. Pushing for reform at the macro, structural level is an example of a crucial area for INGOs to be active in if the analyses of Duffield, Ellis and Keen are to be taken seriously.[33] Lederach's theory of peace-building as a comprehensive array of stages and approaches, incorporating grassroots, middle-level and top-level actors, provides further legitimacy.[34] The complexities of modern conflict predicate the need for a multifarious approach.

However, what is clear is that this peace-building "patchwork" being developed by NGOs and INGOs is not complete; indeed, a crucial piece is missing. The aim of this research, therefore, is to examine critically what generic community-development methodology has to offer in this regard, and how it can be strengthened and consciously used as a peace-building tool. In doing so, it is hoped that NGOs will gain better insight into how to utilize the capacity and resources that we already have. It also aims to help the focus become more long term.

It is important to point out that this research is in no way conclusive. A limited number of ADPs was researched, partly due to the fact that many ADPs are no more than five years old and therefore are not mature enough to be assessed for their impact in this regard. Additionally, this is the first study of its kind, the methodology being developed as the process gathered pace. Another fact to be taken into account is that none of the ADPs studied has yet stood the test of national conflict. All were either set up after a major national conflict or have only experienced local violent conflict. However, this research does provide some strong insights and lessons into principles and approaches, and it should be viewed as an instigator for more work in this area.

Conflict as a product of the abuse of power and "god complexes"

There are many sociological or anthropological theories on the causes of modern violent conflict. However, a Christian philosophy and perspective views this picture as incomplete without a theory that takes into account a more holistic understanding of conflict and its causes—that is, one which includes spiritual factors.

Jayakumar Christian, who has long experience in rural community development in India, has written incisively on this subject.[35] His theories on the nature and causes of intergenerational poverty provide a persuasive and radical understanding of conflict that is particularly helpful to this debate. He argues that systemic poverty is caused and maintained by "god complexes," networks of the powerful that seek to play god in the environment in which they operate (that is, to absolutize themselves, to have ultimate control). These reinforce each other, thus creating power reservoirs and god complexes that the poor, or those without authority, find it impossible to break out of.

Christian uses this concept as a tool by which to understand the dynamics of structural poverty, with particular reference to the Indian subcontinent. However, it is also a powerful model by which to understand the dynamics of power and, by his association, conflict. Several levels and types of conflict emerge from this abuse of power.

First, latent conflict is created between the poor and the rich when the rich exploit the poor and demand their allegiance. An example is the power that moneylenders and landlords have over many communities in rural India. This conflict is rarely expressed and instead usually takes the form of harmony between the exploiter and exploited; the rural poor do not know any different and accept their situation as a natural part of the world order. This sense of "fate" is particularly strong in India, where the caste system dictates position in society. The second type of conflict is overt and emerges when the poor become enlightened about their exploited position. This enlightenment may come through Marxist philosophy (as it did in postwar India), or participatory community development.[36] Third, power that is divisive and relies on the fragmentation of the community also creates conflict for the poor.

Christian's theories are helpful in demonstrating that conflict is an inescapable outcome of the monopoly of power, that conflict is not necessarily expressed, and that it is inherent within structural or systemic inequity. He also demonstrates that relationships are central to an understanding of conflict. To quote Christian: "Humans oppose humans in the struggle to attain, share or influence power" and "An important feature of all poverty situations is broken relationships."

Furthermore, this understanding shows that unequal power relationships and resulting conflict assume a spiritual dimension as god complexes demand extreme control and allegiance in communities—and effectively seek to deify themselves.

In summary, one cannot hope to achieve much in transformational development without recognizing and addressing unequal power relationships. By the same token, one cannot address issues of conflict without looking at the impact of community development on these power relationships.

This thinking defines the philosophy behind transformational development, the vision behind ADPs, and defines our understanding of reconciliation and peace-building.

Civil society

Alan Whaites has pointed out that de Toqueville's understanding of civil society is one which INGOs/NGOs can easily subscribe to—one in which associations are formed primarily for constructive, altruistic concerns to pursue "small issues" (including community development).[37] As a result, they are more likely to form on the basis of these small issues rather than primordial issues such as ethnicity, language and religion, and therefore be a unifying agent for a heterogeneous group.

However, as Whaites argues, what INGOs/NGOs overlook in applying this to community development is that this unifying, positive impact of small-issue groups is not ensured, according to de Toqueville, when the group is homogeneous. This is because it becomes vulnerable to moving on to strengthening the group's comparative position, particularly when in a context of clientism and patronage. Therefore, we should be wary of assuming that all civil associations naturally build civil society.

ADPs, on the other hand, invariably work with a heterogeneous community (due to the size of the area); they depend on the formation of grassroots groups for the different development activities and thus have a strong propensity to develop civil society in both the literal and academic sense of the word.

Oxfam and Saferworld clearly recognize this in the recommendations they made to the European Union on development policies that would help prevent conflict. "EU development cooperation . . . should promote social cohesion by meeting common concerns through programmes which *transcend group interests*" (emphasis added). Furthermore, they suggest that facilitating "the development of representative groups from civil society is a necessary means of contributing to sustainable peace."

Reconciliation as relationship and shalom

Fundamental to any understanding of reconciliation is its dependence on relationship. J. P. Lederach uses this concept as the central tenet of his model of peace-building.[38] According to quantum theory, no system can be understood without examining the relationships of its parts. Reconciliation of those parts, and of that which is causing conflict, must therefore be found through relationship.

Second, encounter is the means by which the building of relationship can take place; a place has to be created for enemies to meet and dialogue.

And third, the focus of this encounter must include dealing with the past and looking to the future. In fact, Lederach says that "envisioning a common future creates new lenses for dealing with the past."

Reconciliation is therefore a locus (physical place) and focus (on each other, on past and future), where relationships are allowed to develop through encounter, and where looking to the future creates new perspectives for dealing with the past. Furthermore, reconciliation is sustained by relationship.

Jayakumar Christian's theory that unjust economic or political relationships are at the root of conflict, whether realized or latent, further supports this understanding of reconciliation. In so doing, it implies that reconciliation may involve deep-seated reform of power structures in order to be true and meaningful. This is, in effect, what participatory development is, or should be, about.

In Christian theology this is articulated as the paradox of justice and mercy meeting. In Christ's teaching, which calls for "a radical love of enemies on the one hand and a forthright confrontation with the perpetrators of injustice on the other," we see this dialectic at work.[39] Lederach's own experience with peace-building work led him to a profound insight into how this works out in real-life reconciliation work. Using the wisdom of Psalm 85:10, he describes how reconciliation is the place where "Truth and Mercy have met together; Peace and Justice have kissed."[40]

This understanding of reconciliation is one that is captured by the Hebrew word *shalom*, which is also frequently misinterpreted. Commonly, it is used to mean "peace"; however, the full interpretation is much richer and originates in the Old Testament account of the creation in Genesis. Here shalom described the perfect state of being that existed among humanity, God and creation, in which each one existed in harmonious and right relationships. Metzler and McAlpine both point out that the unifying theme throughout the Old and New Testaments is of God continually working toward restoring shalom.[41]

When integrated with J. Christian's notion of transformational development being the breaking of god complexes that oppress the poor, we have a holistic understanding of reconciliation that supports the notion that reconciliation and community development are closely integrated.

AREA DEVELOPMENT PROGRAM CONCEPT

Historical context

Area Development Programs (ADPs) were developed in the late 1980s out of the realization by World Vision field offices throughout the world of the advantages of "scaling up" community programs funded through child sponsorship. By covering a larger geographical area and working in a wide number of communities while retaining a micro-level approach, it was seen that community development had the potential to become more integrated and sustainable. This involved addressing the health, socioeconomic, training and educational needs of an administrative district. Macro-issues as well as micro-issues would be addressable, such as improvements to the physical infrastructure, local economy and provision of government services. Moreover, transformational development would have a greater chance of success by encouraging the development of networks and coalitions of community groups so as to mobilize the community to tackle root causes to problems.

In discussion with the fields it was realized that no matter how good the development going on in communities was, it could not be complete.

Communities were not sufficient unto themselves and the causes of poverty were not usually confined to the community context. If their needs were to be adequately met, the context of the area or region in which they were situated must be taken into consideration.[42]

A further advantage in adopting a more integrative approach was the opportunity it created for a more flexible funding approach through a mix of private and public funding. In this way long-term stability can be secured through sponsorship commitments, while short-term, sector-specific government grants allow for specialized assistance and flexibility.

Defining ADPs

It is difficult to define the exact nature of individual ADPs. There is no single comprehensive ADP model or paradigm. Rather, ADPs are a strategy for implementing a development paradigm. They are a framework. Although this paradigm varies according to context, certain fundamental goals and approaches exist in all ADPs.

Similar features

- Promotes integrated community development
- Covers a large, contiguous geographical area
- Is primarily funded by child sponsorship, but sources are multiple
- Has a long-term commitment (10–15 years)
- Makes women and children a priority
- Relies on empowerment, capacity building and participation of stakeholders (beneficiaries and/or local government)
- Emphasizes and builds strategic alliances and networks to impact macro-causes of poverty
- Consists of a process with various stages of intervention, funding and programs aimed at increasing ownership of stakeholders

Variable features

- Nature of bilateral relationship between support and field office
- Geographic size
- Administrative functioning
- Legal status
- Degree of partnership with local government
- Staffing (number of staff, type of roles and interaction with community)
- Structure (number, type and distribution of development committees)
- Transition process (whether it begins as a new project or is a consolidation of several existing projects)[43]

Taking this into account, one can define ADPs as *child-focused, sustainable, transformational development programs covering an area the size of an administrative district, with about 10,000–50,000 people. Activities focus on improvements in health, education, agriculture, micro-enterprise and leadership skills addressed through training, credit provision, infrastructural improvement and capacity building. The operation and community ownership of the ADP largely depends upon a network of committees formed of elected community members who oversee the running of the program at various levels. As a result, the exact approach and nature of the program vary. Facilitators, or village development workers, who are indigenous to the region, are trained and placed in the community to build relationships, mobilize the community, facilitate training, coordinate responsibilities of government extension workers, and encourage networking and cooperation between community leaders and groups. Where Christian churches exist, the facilitator coordinates training and capacity building of church leaders. The time scale is long term, covering a period of 10–15 years.*

ANALYSIS OF RESULTS

As noted at the start of this chapter, presentation of the findings of the research can be found in the full report, where the section on methodology (Appendix A in the full report) explains the choice of indicators. The matrix in Appendix B (in the full report) presents in a more quantitative manner the degree to which each ADP fared.

Indicator One: Increased levels of contact, interaction and communication across geographic, religious, ethnic, cultural and class divides throughout the ADP

General

The type and extent of interaction and communication has markedly improved throughout all levels of the ADP as a direct result of ADP mobilization, projects, meetings, training and infrastructural development. Although the village remains an important focal point for interaction, the parish or *kebele* (Ethiopian lowest level of government administration) has become the most common arena for community activity as a result of the ADP structure, causing new and meaningful interaction among a wider group of people. Interaction beyond the parish level for communal purposes has also arisen for the first time although this is mainly among people who form a minority of the population, that is, committee leaders, elders and trainers.

Ethnic interaction

Tribal interaction is occurring between groups who used not to have contact for any purpose, or as was more common, whose interaction was restricted to trade or occasional community events. This is a direct outcome of the ADP working with entire villages and parishes rather than selected ethnic groups, causing committees and activity groups (such as literacy or micro-enterprise) to be formed that cross ethnic groupings. The level of this interaction is mainly at parish level. However, where networks have been established from the lowest to highest level in the district, as in Omosheleko, frequent communication and decision-making is taking place among tribal elders where this was unprecedented.

Religious

Evidence of formation of friendships and communal decision-making between Muslims and Christians and between Christian denominations abounds in the ADPs. The main influences identified are the all-embracing approach of the ADP, which causes different groups to work together; the exhortation to unity by the staff and mobilizers; and the setting up of local church councils to encourage interdenominational communication.

Class and caste

Interaction among members of the community with different economic or caste backgrounds has certainly improved. However, this varied greatly between ADPs. ADPs have had some impact by bringing local leaders (who are often landlords) and ordinary members of the community together, some uneducated, in committees and development activities. However, this is only having a marked impact where local leaders have significant involvement in the ADP, as in Masaka. Usually, ADPs do not rely on significant participation of landlords and/or leaders, except for purposes of authorization or supervision. As such, their involvement depends on their initiative and interest.

Traditional leaders

Where chiefs, tribal elders and church leaders were actively encouraged to sit on committees and participate in decision-making processes, interaction and dialogue has improved to an unprecedented level. This was found to be the case in all ADPs with the exception of Kwahu in Ghana, where no formal committee had been set up for chiefs to discuss ADP-related issues (in 1998 a chiefs' forum was set up for precisely this purpose).

External organizations: Local government

Communication among the grassroots community and government officials and extension workers depends on the local context and the ADP system. In Kwahu, the ADP relies heavily on cooperation with the government, which is a major stakeholder. Omosheleko ADP deliberately chose to distance itself from the government owing to past experience with the previous government, and so cooperation there is low.

Gender

Male and female interaction has become closer as a result of the ADPs actively encouraging female economic productivity and community service. Women engage in micro-enterprise development activities with the men, attend community meetings and trade with men. The impact on domestic relations was not researched, but from the anecdotal evidence there is a strong indication that this has had a beneficial impact: men are in need of fewer wives now that women are economically productive, resulting in less domestic strife and antagonism among polygamous families. The employment of men in areas where unemployment had been a major problem has also improved family relations.

However, it must be pointed out that the degree of involvement by women in community-development decisions has been limited in that female representation on development committees is very low. Masaka, where it was stipulated that at least three committee members be women, was the exception.[44] As a result women are more active in decision-making. Increased female productivity and participation in Uganda is a national phenomenon, though this was not found to be the case in the Kwahu or Omosheleko region.

Indicator Two: Improved cooperation, unity and interdependence

Tribal and sectarian mistrust, prejudice and independence dramatically eroded and community relations deepened

Throughout each ADP evidence abounded of the development of trust, understanding, concern, unity, confidence and dependence between ethnic and religious groups. This was probably the most overt change in attitudes witnessed, second to attitudes toward health and self-development. Tribes that had previously lived together but held deep mistrust of one another for centuries were expressing mutual respect and concern for each other, while church division appeared to be a thing of the past in all the ADPs. This was most profound in Masaka, where Catholic and Protestant mutual suspicion has been rife for over a century. Similar trends are occurring in Uganda as a whole; however, these changes appear to be much stronger in the ADP.

An additional important insight was the fact that the ADP had taught communities that the cause of their poverty or problems was not necessarily related to their ethnic or religious status.

No less important has been the strengthening of teaching in the local Christian churches, which has arisen as a direct result of church leadership capacity building. One of the outcomes has been preaching that is inclusive and embracing of others rather than divisive.

Progressive attitudes are emerging toward stigmatized groups and lower classes, though change is not always dramatic

Masaka and Omosheleko ADPs both demonstrated progressive behavior and attitudes toward lower classes and castes, respectively, which consequently deserve mention. In Omosheleko, the treatment of *fugas*, who have been traditional outcasts for centuries, has shown definite improvement that exceeds the change that is occurring nationally. In certain communities *fugas* have been allowed to assume leadership positions, attend meetings and drink coffee with non-*fugas*. Yet this is not universal within the ADP, with some *fugas* still being stigmatized and none holding leadership positions on decision-making committees.

Masaka is the only ADP out of the five visited (including the pilot studies) that attempted to include members of different economic *and* gender classes on one committee. Phulbani ADP in India (included in the pilot study) was exemplary in the way it attempted to include all caste groups in the village on the same committee, but it separated men and women. Even so, it is an excellent example of how insisting on representative committees has paid off—caste barriers within the village were dramatically eroded and reconciliation of enemies occurred (see section below entitled "Transformation of community dynamics, breaking of caste and religious ancient barriers and reconciliation of enemies").

Community ownership and declining levels of dependency are variable and depend on the effectiveness of the mobilizer and development committees

Overall, enthusiasm for the work and attendance at meetings was good, and committees were active and effective. The health and economic status of participants was much improved. However, degrees of dependency, shown in loan repayment rates and the questionable commitment of some committees, varied within the ADPs and could not be said to be a thing of the past (although improvements had certainly been made). Those areas that were remarkable for their initiative and vision were usually those that had capable, energetic village development workers/mobilizers and also had representative committees that were supported by the entire community, traditional leaders included.

Spirit of service and sacrifice

Demonstrations of the degree of understanding and respect that has grown between heterogeneous groups tended to be found in those same communities where community ownership had taken hold. Such communities were prompted to carry sick *fugas* to the hospital, to build a house for AIDS orphans without village development worker prompting, and for Catholics to drive a Muslim sheikh to the airport on his way to Mecca.

Openness to outsiders and communal celebration

One of the community-based indicators set during the pilot research was an improved attitude toward outsiders. This was definitely found in Kwahu and Masaka, as demonstrated by desires for a guest house and the preparation of a meal for the team. The role of communal celebration was not discovered through the visits as they were during the pilot research—attendance of weddings and social visits tended to be on the decline because of the increased demands on time that the development activities had placed on community members. The welcome received at Phulbani ADP and the extent of hospitality experienced there were exceptional.

Reduction of unsociable habits

Many ADP communities mentioned the fact that drunkenness was no longer a problem, though this was not the case in control groups. The decline was not as dramatic as that in Phulbani, although it must be admitted that the problem was extremely serious there.

Improvement in resolution of local conflicts and reduction in number of petty conflicts

Each culture within the ADPs has its own distinct way of dealing with local conflicts. Certain evidence points to how the ADP system of social organization has improved the ability of rural communities to resolve these conflicts.

First, in Omosheleko, local level chiefs pointed out that they no longer spend so much time visiting villages to mediate and pass judgment over communal issues. The reason given was that villages are now sorting out the problems themselves.

In Kwahu, fighting over access to water sources (which had increased in number but consequently attracted more users) had been sorted out. In another case traditional bickering over common land boundaries no longer occurred as the community developed a more cooperative mentality.

These examples indicate that the establishment of the village development committee and the mobilization of the community to attempt to resolve its own problems have increased local capacity to deal with these small resource-based problems.

In the case of the serious conflict over the land boundary in Omosheleko in 1994, the setting up of the elders council in the late 1980s (pre-ADP) to oversee the relief and rehabilitation program proved to be a highly useful preparation for the deliberations in 1994, which elders from the two tribes involved were required to preside over. By this stage they had become familiar with cooperative decision-making and some had developed friendships ("We kiss each other," according to the elder). As a result they were better equipped for such a process. The ADP manager was even asked to coordinate the meetings. As a result, the steering committee had become an ad hoc conflict management committee.[45]

Sharing of vision, experience, resources and ideas— economies of scale and social capital

The potential for more effective economies of scale was demonstrated by Phulbani ADP, whose Apex committees have provided a valuable channel through which financially stronger credit unions can be formed and larger agricultural machinery bought. Their multiplying effect was alluded to by several community members. More important, now leaders have the stimulus for greater cooperation between communities beyond the village level and the confidence to advocate for improved services from the local government and better agricultural prices.

This collective energy was not deliberately engineered or directed by the ADP staff. Instead, it came as a natural progression of the mobilizing and organizational work of the ADP.

Indications of solidarity and interdependence rising above politics exist but are not conclusive

Despite the fact that this cooperative energy is not fully realized, a strong degree of ADP-wide solidarity and interdependence has been identified by the community itself in Omosheleko and hinted at in Masaka.

In the former, senior committee members spoke of how the inclusive, participatory approach of an ADP that is run by a neutral or nongovernmental body has had a tremendous impact on the attitude of tribes toward each other, building up solidarity among them. They even mentioned that it has, to a certain extent, begun to reverse the effect of the government's ethnicization policy.

In Masaka, the confession in the control groups that recent political developments were causing sectarian and ethnic division to reemerge was not echoed in the ADP, indicating a small but crucial degree of difference in the changes in relationships in Masaka ADP.

These insights indicate a capacity within ADPs to bring about a level of solidarity that can rise above divisive politics. However, the evidence is not sufficient to be conclusive. More time is required to see how the ADPs will fare in the next few years.

Additional insights from the pilot research

Some of the findings from the study of Phulbani and Chowfaldani ADPs in India have been alluded to in the above section. However, some important points have not been mentioned. Although the study of these ADPs was not measured against control groups, some of the findings were very compelling.

Transformation of community dynamics, breaking of caste and religious ancient barriers and reconciliation of enemies

In Phulbani, untouchables had been integrated into the social norms of the village, with all but Brahmins eating with them; higher-caste tribes now choose to sit behind the lower caste whose village they are visiting, a sign of deference; enemy villages that had violent conflicts in the past over resources now worked together and embraced each other. In Nutunmahl Village, Chowfaldani, the unprecedented cooperation of orthodox Muslims and Hindus for development activities has prompted changes not found in other parts of the ADP: eating at one another's festivals and the relaxation of many *purdah* restrictions.

Role of village development worker (VDW)

The common thread in both cases was the quality and example of the village development workers and the degree of self-reliance and participation that was encouraged from the start. Phulbani used a highly participatory process whereby VDWs lived with the communities for up to two years, developing trust and encouraging unity and cooperation before introducing development activities. All the communities in question pointed to the role model of the VDW in improving their attitude toward their neighbors and their self-development. They were referring to the way VDWs treated them with equal respect, were trustworthy and spent time with those not of their faith as well as their own.

Advocacy role of Apex groups

Apex coalitions, which are the equivalent to cluster communities in Kwahu and zonal committees in Omosheleko, were particularly vibrant in Phulbani and demonstrated the multiplying effect that they can have. As discussed earlier, the communities are using these coalitions to their full advantage by accessing large loans through them, obtaining licenses for development activity from local authorities and organizing large social events. However, their advocacy role is also one they have begun to use to overcome broader, less immediate problems—Apex leaders themselves began to deal with government authorities directly to obtain services to which the community is entitled and to raise the issue of low agricultural prices.

ADPs accelerating and extrapolating national and regional trends

The main finding of the control-group studies was that many of the trends found in the ADPs were confirmed to be national and regional trends, but that the ADP had the effect of considerably reinforcing these trends.

Where the ADP had a considerably different impact on regional trends was in Omosheleko and Phulbani. In the former, assertion of ethnic identity is the norm, in contrast to the situation in the ADP area. In Orissa State and throughout the northeast of India, Hindu fundamentalism is on the increase. This is in contrast to Phulbani, where antagonism toward Christianity has substantially declined. The community has experienced first-hand that Christianity is not a threat to them.

PRINCIPLE PEACE-BUILDING CATALYSTS

Formation of heterogeneous community-development groups and committees at various levels throughout the ADP

The operation of each ADP revolves around a network of committees and activity groups through whom and around which development activities are organized and channeled. The extent and type of these groups varies for each ADP; however, the basic principle exists in all. Such groups are fundamental to the mobilization of the community and to creating a structure within which the mobilized community can participate. More important, such groups create a forum for interaction and cooperation among a cross-section of the community, thereby drawing together groups who would not traditionally have met or collaborated for common economic or social goals. These groups are providing opportunities for dialogue, the development of trust, shared futures and, most important, dependence on one another. Consequently, erosion of prejudice, developing of mutual friendships and common understanding and, in some cases, reconciliation is occurring.

The degree to which these groups encourage cooperation and interdependence among heterogeneous people groups depends on three factors: (1) the way in which the groups are formed or elected, that is, how representative they are; (2) the distribution of people groups throughout the ADP area; and (3) the extent of the network (village through to district).

All-embracing approach and impartiality of World Vision

A number of factors relating to the development organization's nongovernmental status and impartial approach were "unifying."

First, the fact that assistance was inclusive, targeting all ethnic, religious and social groups alike, spoke deeply to the communities of the need for impartiality. This message is particularly powerful when the community is aware that the agency is a Christian-based organization.

Second, the organization's encouragement and, where necessary, demand that the different communities work together without prejudice and in unity, introduced unprecedented ways of thinking into the ADP community.

Third, the organization's nongovernmental status and lack of alignment with any particular people group or political party rendered it a powerful "unifying agent" (to quote a local person in Omosheleko ADP) in its management of the intergroup activities. This is particularly crucial in contexts where the government (whether past or present) has been associated with division and war.

Finally, it was noticed that those ADPs that work closely with the government (such as Kwahu) are those that tend to have a much smaller impact on unifying groups. This is not only because the approach is usually more "top-down," and therefore generates less interdependence between the communities, but because the ADP is more closely associated with local government.

Role and example of village development workers in transforming attitudes and values

The role of the VDWs in Phulbani ADP and Chowfaldandi ADP in influencing community attitudes was found to be particularly significant. Although both of these ADPs were studied as pilot studies, the function and role of their VDWs are markedly different from those found in the other three ADPs and as such deserve special attention.

The VDWs were crucial not only to the success of the project in terms of facilitating community development, but also in transforming community attitudes, values and perceptions. Significant evidence points to the example of their lifestyle, which promoted the values of tolerance, humility, faithfulness, self-sacrifice, service and nondiscrimination. Such a "lifestyle approach" laid the foundation for cooperation and respect of diverse groups that held greater power than verbal teaching.

However, the value of verbal exhortation has also been shown to be significant by way of the leadership training sessions given by community workers to committee leaders. These sessions included teaching on the values of integrity, honesty, service, fairness, respect for one another, and forgiveness.

The example and teaching have clearly had a significant impact on the reconciliation of former enemies, a willingness to cross divides and listen to one another, and a fundamental respect for diverse communities.

This understanding of the crucial role of values in the development process is one that has been recognized over the years.[46] These findings on the influential role of the VDW in this regard not only affirms this thinking but also demonstrates their utility in any peace-building initiatives.

However, a note of caution must be made with regard to placing too much emphasis on a system that relies too heavily on individuals. Should a situation arise where a VDW has less pure motives or standards, or where he or she leaves abruptly, the success of the program in the area will be jeopardized. To prevent this, systems and checks must be put in place to ensure that the community does not become overly reliant on the VDW.

Strengthening of local churches through capacity building and leadership training

Kwahu and Omosheleko ADPs are both set within contexts where the Christian church is predominant and is growing dramatically. Consequently, the program design took into account the need to increase the capacity of local churches, both in leadership and mobilization skills and in interrelations.

The impact has been fourfold:

- a big increase in numbers attending church, leading to
- increased interaction occurring at church between traditionally noninteractive people groups
- teaching that is embracing and inclusive rather than divisive, and
- unity among churches that is unprecedented.

The implications this has for peace-building is twofold: first, reconciliation is beginning to take place between groups and churches that formerly were divided, and second, an attitude of tolerance and brotherly love is being developed throughout the community, strengthening relationships across groups. Where Christianity is the majority religion (as in southern Ghana, southern Ethiopia and Uganda) and the church is a respected local association, this is a highly significant development, raising the potential for future stability and cohesion.

Examples of reconciliation include the Muslim and Christian community in Hwee Hwee, Kwahu ADP, where relations were once strained and prejudice high, largely as a result of divisive church teaching and lack of cooperation on development issues. In Omosheleko, the multifarious local churches are now freely mixing and holding joint services, where previously fierce enmity existed. Furthermore, church members are beginning to treat outcasts with greater respect as they now share the same pew with them and are being taught the biblical truths of equality in Christ. It must be noted, however, that this is not universal in the ADP, with problems unfortunately still occurring in this regard. However, progress is being made that is directly attributable to improvements in church teaching.

APPENDIX

Indicators of improved relations among and within heterogeneous communities

Increased levels of contact, interaction and communication

Throughout the ADP (parish, village, sub-center, zone and district level) to the extent that there is a *regular* and *voluntary* interaction for *social or community* purposes where previously interaction had been limited or purely for economic reasons.

Improved cooperation, unity, trust and interdependence

Throughout the ADP (parish, village, sub-center, zone and district level) to the extent that attitudes between groups have become inclusive, prejudices eroded, trust developed and dependence on one another initiated and sustained.

These indicators are examined

- between religious groups
- between ethnic groups or tribes
- between classes or castes
- between men and women
- between community chiefs and leaders
- between the community and external organizations (government agencies, NGOs, commercial businesses)

Detailed indicators for each ADP varied owing to each context being unique, but the main generic ones are listed below:

Within kebeles:

- active and effective community mobilization and development action
- enthusiasm demonstrated by community for community organized activities
- active and enthusiastic village development committees and subcommittee groups
- "dependency spirit" lessened
- financial accountability demonstrated by village development committees
- regular attendance at community meetings
- cooperation of whole community/different groups in community initiatives*

- participation of minority groups in decision-making processes/representative village committees
- respect for credit unions shown through repayment of loans
- community initiative and vision (formation of new groups or activities)
- increased socialization among different groups and communities (attending funerals, weddings, eating with one another)
- strengthening of relations between community leaders (religious and traditional)*
- reconciliation of long-standing enemies/resolution of past conflicts
- improved family/gender relations
- improved efficacy of problem-solving structures
- spirit of service and self-sacrifice, and sharing*
- regular interaction among churches and religious groups
- open attitude toward outsiders*

Within clusters of kebeles:

- active, fair and representative committees that are respected by the entire community
- minority groups participating in the decision-making process
- enthusiasm by members for committees and their work
- members from different villages/towns developing relationships with one another
- communities willingly engaging in joint activities*
- committees respected and supported by communities, most especially chiefs and leaders with whom cooperation exists
- good understanding and relations among leaders (religious and traditional)*
- cooperation with government officials and staff on local programs and improved rapport between the people and government officials
- increased socialization between different groups and communities (attending funerals, weddings, eating with one another)
- effective management of conflicts
- no bias or prejudice expressed toward one part of community
- positive attitudes toward different groups and villages (in religious, ethnic and caste status)*
- reconciliation of long-standing enemies/resolution of past conflicts
- improved efficacy of problem-solving structures
- regular interaction between churches and religious groups

* *Indicators identified by communities during pilot research.*

Notes

[1] NCDO, *From Early Warning to Early Action: A Report on the European Conference on Conflict Prevention*, ed. Dutch Center for Conflict Prevention (NCDO Publications, 1997).

[2] J. P. Lederach, *Building Peace: Sustainable Reconciliation in Divided Societies* (Washington, D.C.: United States Institute of Peace Press, 1997), 4–5. Lederach bases his conclusion on statistics from a number of sources, most notable being Peter Wallensteen and Karin Axell, *Armed Conflict at the End of the Cold War 1989–92* (1993), *Journal of Peace Research* 30, no. 3; and Stockholm International Peace Research Institute (SIPRI) Yearbook: *World Armaments and Disarmament* (New York: Humanities Press, 1995).

[3] E. Regehr, *After the Cold War: Shaping a Canadian Response*, Ploughshares Working Paper (1993), cited in Lederach, *Building Peace*.

[4] Ibid., 65.

[5] The number of refugees has soared since 1960 with 16 million refugees in 1995 as compared with 2.5 million in 1960. Source: United Nations Development Program, Human Development Report 1997, 66.

[6] See Lederach, *Building Peace*; Larry Minear and Thomas G. Weiss, *Mercy Under Fire* (Boulder, Colo.: Westview Press, 1995); Carnegie Commission on Preventing Deadly Conflict, final report, Carnegie Corporation of New York (December 1997).

[7] This view is propounded by Duffield in "Warlords, Post-Adjustment Rulers and Private Protection," paper presented at a Disasters Emergency Conclusion seminar in London, February 1998.

[8] One of the conclusions of the Relief and Rehabilitation Network paper "Humanitarian Action in Protracted Crises: The New Relief 'Agenda' and Its Limits" by Dylan Hendrickson. The paper is a synthesis of the outcomes of the DEC seminar in London, February 1998.

[9] Notably by authors such as Alex de Waal. See his *Humanitarianism Unbound? African Rights* (1994) and *Famine Crimes* (1998).

[10] For an understanding of these types of "diplomacy," see International Alert's discussion paper, "Towards a Policy Framework for Advancing Preventive Diplomacy" by K. Rupesinghe (1995); and chapter 1 of the 1998 NCDO Directory *Prevention and Management of Violent Conflicts: An International Directory*.

[11] For an interesting analysis, see Douglas Johnston and Cynthia Sampson, eds., *Religion: The Missing Dimension of Statecraft* (New York: Oxford University Press, 1994).

[12] Mary Anderson's paper "Do No Harm: Supporting Local Capacities for Peace Through Aid" and work through the Local Capacities for Peace Initiative have championed this philosophy. Anderson seeks to encourage humanitarian agencies to analyze how their interventions affect local dynamics and to draw on local capacities that have the ability to build peace.

[13] One example of such advocacy initiatives is the European Union and Conflict Forum, which comprises a group of specialist and operational UK NGOs lobbying the UK and European Union governments to introduce policies that are more sensitive to internal conflicts around the world. A European Union code of conduct on arms trade is currently being lobbied for.

[14] This thinking formed the basis of World Vision Bosnia's decision in 1997 to adopt a deliberate peace-building dimension to its reconstruction work.

[15] Most UK NGOs state that they believe conflict is an inherent part of social change and not necessarily negative. However, due to the common use of the word *conflict* to mean "violent conflict," the perception is created that conflict is inherently negative.

[16] K. Bush, "Beyond Bungee Cord Humanitarianism: Towards a Developmental Agenda for Peace-building," *Canadian Journal of Development Studies* (Special Issue 1996), 14.

[17] Eric Ram and David Westwood, *NGOs and Reconciliation: Rebuilding Communities* (Geneva: World Vision Liaison Office, 1996).

[18] From introductory remarks by Robert Dodd in *Understanding Peace and Conflict Management*, report from ActionAid workshop in Ghana (1995).

[19] See *Prevention and Management of Violent Conflicts: An International Directory*, 23.

[20] World Vision International, *Reconciliation Commission Report to the World Vision Council* (September 1998), 59.

[21] Carl Lane, in *Anthropology in Action* (1996).

[22] E. Voutira and S. Whisthaw Brown, *Conflict Resolution: A Cautionary Tale*, Refugee Studies Programme (1995), 25.

[23] A. Carl, "Supporting Local Capacities for Handling Violent Conflict: A Role for International NGOs?," in *Anthropology in Action* 3, no. 3 (Winter 1996).

[24] Ram and Westwood, *NGOs and Reconciliation*.

[25] See "Assumptions" section in *World Vision Bosnia Framework for Reconciliation and Peace-building* (1997).

[26] These are the two-year Institute for Development Policy and Management (University of Manchester, UK) project, NGOs and Peace-building in CPEs (Complex Political Emergencies); the three-year COPE (Complex Political Emergencies Project), also an NGO-academic cooperation; and the Overseas Development Institute (ODI) review of evaluation studies of peace-building projects.

[27] See Overseas Development Institute (ODI), *A Manual on Alternative Conflict Management for Community-Based Natural Resource Projects in the South Pacific: Context, Principles, Tools and Training Materials* (June 1998).

[28] M. Warner and P. Jones, "Assessing the Need to Manage Conflict in Community-based Natural Resource Projects," *Natural Resource Perspectives* 35, ODI (1998).

[29] The definition of *peace-building* and its application with regard to ADPs is dealt with comprehensively in the section entitled "Spirit of Service and Sacrifice" below. For now, it suffices to say that I use it in the broadest sense of the word, implying initiatives that develop a culture of peace, whether deliberately or as a byproduct of a different activity, and can be either before, during or after conflict.

[30] Bush, "Beyond Bungee Cord Humanitarianism," 14.

[31] For example, see Oxfam and Saferworld, "The Future of EU-ACP Relations and Conflict Prevention" (1997), Oxfam International Position Paper on the Great Lakes (1998), the Machel Study on Children in Armed Conflict; UN Secretary General report on *The Causes of Conflict and the Promotion of Durable Peace* (1998); and Geraldine McDonald, *Peace-building from Below* (1997).

[32] M. Renner, in T. Spencer, *Preliminary Synthesis of Peace-building Evaluations*, Humanitarian Policy Group, ODI (1998).

[33] These leading development political economists argue that the loss of the control of the state in the face of globalization, liberalization and decentralization has directly contributed to the emergence of private, predatory actors who wage war to gain control of key markets. As such, these forces are the key instigators of violent conflict. See M. Duffield, "Complex Emergencies and the Crisis of Develop-

mentalism," *IDS Bulletin: Linking Relief and Development* 25, no. 4 (October 1994).

[34] Lederach, *Building Peace*.

[35] Jayakumar Christian, "An Alternate Reading of Poverty," chapter 1 herein; and idem, "A Different Way to Look at Poverty" in *Body and Soul*, an edited version of papers presented at the second World Vision Christian Forum, London, May 1998.

[36] The need for managing this process with sensitivity and integrating the non-poor into the process is recognized and seen as essential if violent conflict is not to be a consequence of this enlightenment.

[37] A. Whaites, "Let's Get Civil Society Straight: NGOs and Political Theory," *Development in Practice* 6, no. 3 (1996), 240.

[38] See Lederach, *Building Peace*.

[39] See H. Wells, in G. Baum and H. Wells, *The Reconciliation of the Peoples: Challenge to the Churches* (Geneva: World Council of Churches, 1997), chap. 1.

[40] See Lederach, *Building Peace*, 28–29.

[41] James E. Metzler, *From Saigon to Shalom* (Scottdale, Pa.: Herald Press, 1995); and see Joy Alvarez, Elnora Avarientos and Thomas H. McAlpine, chapter 4 herein.

[42] World Vision Australia, *ADP Final Report* (April 1995).

[43] The ADP in Masaka began as an orphan-assistance program. It was therefore considered important that women participate in decision-making.

[44] Andrew Natsios discusses this case in I. Zartman and L. Rasmussen, *International Conflict: Methods and Techniques* (Washington, D.C.: U.S. Institute of Peace Press, 1996).

[45] Explorations on the role of ethics and values in community development have been discussed in a number of documents by authors such as Denis Goulet, "Development: Creator and Destroyer of Values," *World Development* 20, no. 3 (March 1992); Des Gasper, *Development Ethics—An Emergent Field?*, Working Paper Series no. 134 (The Hague: Institute of Social Studies); and Ted Vandeloo, *Responsibility for the Future: Christian Ethics and Social Change* (London: Global Ethics Network, 1987). Of particular note is A. K. Giri's paper "Rethinking the Imperative of Responsibility: Development Ethics, Aesthetics and the Challenge of Poverty" (Madras Institute of Development Studies, 1998), which argues the need for self-development of the *agent* of development. This is one that has been neglected but is essential to the process of development.

8

Engaging in Relationships
with the Business Sector

CORINA VILLACORTA

Nongovernmental organizations (NGOs) are challenged by a context of increasing poverty and vulnerability on the one hand, and excessive concentration of wealth on the other. Both situations are expressions of capitalism at a global stage and are emerging in different settings in the North and South, in the East and West. This phenomenon demands a revision of some assumptions about the promotion of development. I suggest that NGOs must explore possible development frontiers and engage in creative relationships with business organizations, namely private enterprises, corporations, companies and private firms at the local, national and international level.[1] These relationships should be pursued beyond the need for fundraising and traditional advocacy work.

Overcoming old dichotomies and searching for a new synthesis are imperative in discovering new approaches to transformational development. Today's technological revolution is having a tremendous impact on the making of societies, the global economy and the different types of relationships emerging at various levels among many actors. The world is integrating at an incredible pace due to technology and communication stimulating the flow of people, goods and capital in an increasingly interconnected world. These phenomena require us to integrate our frameworks, approaches and methods. In light of this, relationships with business organizations are much more than adding yet another program to the operations of NGOs. Indeed, there is a temptation to seek relationships with business organizations only as another strategy with high potential for more effective fund-raising at a time when resources from traditional sources and methods are scarce. The main purpose in establishing this relationship, however, should be to make a more significant impact in the different areas of the world in which NGOs are actively present (Villacorta 1997a).

A PROPOSED FRAME OF REFERENCE AND RATIONALE

Let me begin by proposing a frame of reference and rationale for engaging in creative relationships with the business sector. The first idea to consider is that development under the existing capitalist system is uneven, inconstant and nonlinear (see Storper and Walker 1989). This is especially evident in the present stage of globalization. Stephen Commins writes:

> The commonly used term "globalization" often obscures as much as it describes, but its core meaning in terms of an increasingly integrated global economy at the level of financial flows, investment, technology, information, and communication systems is essentially true. What is often missing in the discussion of global trends is that beneath the wide sweeping flows of change are enormous dislocations, large populations that are either marginal to the process or losing ground into deeper levels of poverty (Commins 1997, 1).

Globalization is having both a positive and negative impact on the lives of people across the globe, regardless of their geographic location. This phenomenon calls for a more comprehensive understanding of the problems of poverty, increasing vulnerabilities and the damage to the environment. The commonly used terms *development/underdevelopment, First and Third Worlds, rich and poor nations* are not sufficient to describe more complex and changing realities. Seers's statement at the Society for International Development in 1969 is still relevant:

> "The questions to ask about a country's development are therefore: What has been happening to poverty? What has been happening to unemployment? What has been happening to inequality? If all three of these have declined from high levels, then beyond doubt this has been a period of development for the country concerned. If one or two of these central problems have been growing worse, especially if all three have, it would be strange to call the result 'development,' even if per capita income doubled" (cited in Friedmann 1980, 164).

The second idea to consider is that NGOs are only one actor in promoting development. The importance of NGOs has grown significantly during the last two decades, during which they have gained recognition from governments, the media and international organizations such as the UN and the World Bank. This recognition, however, has not exempted NGOs from serious questions and critiques about their effectiveness in fostering development efforts. There are other actors whose roles are even more important: governments, the business/private sector, churches, community groups and grassroots movements, and multilateral organizations, among others.

For almost five decades NGOs have been active in promoting alternative types of development, partnering specifically with poor communities, churches and grassroots groups. Most NGOs emerged as anti-government organizations but over time have established a level of cooperation with governments, especially at the local level. Lately NGOs have occasionally replaced government in some of its social and economic functions. For the purpose of promoting development, NGOs emphasized the necessity of working mainly with the poor, grassroots organizations and governments (see Korten 1990; Friedmann 1992; Edwards and Hulme 1994). What has been absent in this approach is a discussion of how to go about establishing relationships with the business sector. An alternative approach to development has not considered a direct relationship with major economic and political actors in the making of the capitalist system in which the search for development takes place. Historically, most NGOs, especially in the North, have related to the business sector mainly in terms of charity work and advocacy. The business sector, for the most part, has been omitted in most of the proposals, rhetoric and practice of NGOs, with the exception of the two types of interaction already mentioned.

The context of poverty and the concentration of wealth

Poverty and inequalities are expanding even in unexpected places, such as in advanced industrialized societies (see De Brie 1996; Petras and Cavaluzi 1996). In less industrialized societies, inequalities are deepening, submerging new sectors under poverty conditions and new social vulnerabilities. In Eastern European countries a whole new set of unforeseen problems has opened up, and additional needs emerge as societies make a transition to free market oriented economies. The complexity of the problems that various societies face today is challenging previous assumptions and ways of understanding social and economic development, highlighting the need for collaboration and dialogue at different levels among various actors: governments, businesses, grassroots groups and NGOs.

As Alan Fowler states, "Inequality in wealth distribution and economic growth rates has been widening both within and between continents, countries and citizens. Despite international aid, the poor are increasing in absolute and proportional terms" (1997, 216). In this context it is interesting to observe how concerns regarding poverty issues have changed during the last decade, particularly in wealthier nations. Poverty in the South and East is seen not only as a problem for those societies but as a source of international instability and insecurity, which aid can help to neutralize. "Today, we are dealing with a case of aid as enlightened Northern preventive self-defense, not a moral obligation of rich to poor. So it is in the interest of the poor and of corporations that a more pragmatic approach to aid and development is taking place. Corporations want profit and the rich want stability" (ibid.). This is true not only at the international level. Corporations and the rich in both industrialized and less-industrialized societies are increasingly concerned with the domestic poor and vulnerabilities regarding poverty issues such as crime, delinquency, drug addiction and insecurity.

The expansion of poverty runs parallel to the concentration of wealth. There is more research available about poverty than there is about wealth and how it is both concentrating and expanding. But there is evidence of wealth concentration in both rich and poor nations. A new balance is needed in the distribution of wealth, and mechanisms should be created to procure this, along with appropriate questions about the means by which this wealth is created, especially when it is at the expense of increasing poverty. The relationship with the business sector, especially with large and powerful corporations and enterprises, should serve also to gain better distribution of wealth and fairer methods for production and trade.

The new role of the state, the market and civil society

Privatizing social services is currently a common policy being implemented by governments around the globe. As governments withdraw from social responsibility and diminish welfare services, private organizations are supposed to assume some of these roles. This is happening at a time of rising poverty and inequalities in industrialized countries and less industrialized ones, as well as in societies in transition. Not only must governments respond to new and emerging problems of the new poor, the unemployed and the excluded, but business organizations are also being pressed to respond. Although NGOs as a part of civil society are not pressed in the same ways governments and business organizations are, they are also expected to fulfill more effective roles, specifically in international aid and cooperation matters.

NGOs are also expected to help fill the gap left by a diminishing welfare state. More than ever, governments and the public are demanding that NGOs be held accountable and improve their performance. The growing importance of NGOs worldwide has been accompanied by increased pressure for efficiency and concrete results. This demand also comes increasingly from the grassroots. It is no news that NGOs are undergoing increasing scrutiny (see Brandt 1997).

The market has grown to have a tremendous importance in the lives of people around the globe. More and more the poor are entering into market activities both in urban settings and in traditional rural areas. Some argue for market rights as a way out of exclusion from an increasingly integrated economy. Eastern European societies demand support for their transition to market economies and integration into the global market. But the market is not always fair to everyone; neither is it neutral terrain. Markets are neither static nor predetermined. Different forces are at play, and while business organizations are key players, producers and consumers as well as national and international regulators are also important. It is difficult to think about promoting development without influencing the market. What is the role of NGOs in all of this? This is a question to be answered within each particular context. There are no rules, for markets vary from context to context. But the need to influence is obvious if significant transformations are to be promoted.

International aid and cooperation are moving away from a model that relied on the state as organizer and provider, to a model that makes demands on the market, specifically on business organizations. This is happening in the midst of a redefinition of the role of the state and increased power of business organizations.

The business sector and the increasing sense of corporate social responsibility

I do not intend to provide a comprehensive definition of the business sector, but I wish to highlight some characteristics and present roles that are relevant to promoting transformational development.

Business organizations, regardless of their size and type of activity, exist to make profit and accumulate as much as possible. Profit-making and competition are the engines of these organizations, and their operations produce both positive and negative outcomes for people and the environment (Kolodner 1994). Business organizations participate in a wide range of economic activities: production (both extraction and manufacture), agriculture and industry, services in different areas and commercial and financial activities. Business organizations have been key in bringing about technological changes, economic growth, access to new products and innovations, including those produced in the management field and in the making of modern organizations. On the other hand, the search to maximize profit has led business organizations to exploit child labor, damage the environment, promote unhealthy consumption of food and pharmaceutical products and other negative practices. Because of their modest contribution in social matters and the increasingly negative consequences of their activities to society, there is a growing demand from different sectors for business organizations to fulfill a responsible social role (Kolodner 1994; Estes 1996).

Business organizations participate in society at different levels. Some participate at local and regional levels, others have a national scope, and the largest ones participate at the transnational level. National and transnational corporations have gained tremendous power and importance. Increasingly influential on a global scale, transnational corporations have grown into very complex organizations about which there is insufficient understanding in the NGO community.

Corporations and financial institutions, particularly those that are transnational, have gained unexpected privileges and power, some of them managing resources greater than those of nation-states (Korten 1995; Kolodner 1994). They have become a cosmopolitan elite with more power than governments or other modern organizations, not to mention NGOs. The power and resources transnational corporations have make them bear responsibility toward societies and environments in which they act, and also make them accountable to governments and civil societies.

The notion of corporate social responsibility emerged in the last half of the twentieth century, mainly in the United States. There is a long tradition of both philanthropy and corporate social responsibility in the United States. Beginning in the 1960s, adverse public opinion began to rise against business in that country. The value of ever-increasing production, with its resultant pollution and environmental decay, and defective products and services came under question from a more critical public.

The sentiment for corporate social responsibility is increasing in other countries, both in the North and the South, for example, in Australia,[2] the Netherlands,[3] Costa Rica,[4] and Peru.[5] In Europe, Germany and the Netherlands lead in matters of corporate social responsibility. Brazil is the country with the longest tradition of corporate giving in Latin America. The total amount of corporate giving exceeded significantly the amount of money spent by NGOs in Brazil during the mid-1990s (De Oliveira and Tandon 1994).

It is important that NGOs position themselves strategically to participate in the expansion of the notion of corporate social responsibility. Moreover, NGOs could help deepen that notion by facilitating the involvement of business organizations in poverty alleviation and transformational development efforts.

The role of international development cooperation and NGOs

NGOs are an important component of the international cooperation and aid system. Since their inception, NGOs have engaged in different practices to promote alternative types of development that favor the poor, the oppressed and the excluded. Recently, however, questions have been asked about the effectiveness of the whole aid system and particularly the role of NGOs, because poverty is expanding despite the large amounts of money spent in international cooperation aimed at alleviating it. This is one reason NGOs are experiencing a reduction in funding for their work in international cooperation matters.

Increasing poverty in industrialized societies makes it more difficult for NGOs to access funds from governments to supply aid to poor countries. This trend is taking place in Canada, the United States and Europe (see Kelleher and McLaren 1996; Van der Ploeg and Sap 1995; Comalieu 1996).

This is another reason NGOs now look to the corporate sector as an alternative source for funding. Indeed, the corporate sector in those areas has tremendous potential for funding, but the reality is that many corporations, at least in the United States, Australia and the Netherlands, are more interested in funding domestic programs.[6] Some corporations with transnational operations, however, are also interested in supporting programs in poorer countries.

Latin American NGOs are experiencing a reduction in funding from their counterparts in the North, and so are turning to their own national private enterprises as an alternative source for funding. They engage in different types of relationships with business organizations, and participate directly in for-profit operations themselves (Villacorta 1997b).

The NGO community is at a critical stage. As previously noted, not only is it experiencing a reduction in funding from traditional sources but it is also under a more critical lens regarding performance. And at the same time NGOs are expected to fill the gap that governments leave behind as they pull back from their social and economic responsibilities.

The corporate mentality has been permeating NGO practice, particularly during the 1990s. At the same time, business organizations, due in part to their need to compete and to pressures from different sectors of civil society, are starting to acknowledge that there are some things they can learn from NGOs. We are talking here of two different sets of values, missions and perhaps even of conflicting interests. There are two perspectives and two types of organizations playing different roles in society. It is important to remain aware of the differences. At the same time the current global situation calls for a search for common ground.

SOME WORLD VISION EXPERIENCES

The traditional relationship with business organizations

World Vision offices, mainly in the United States and Canada, have spent many years in establishing relationships with corporations. The most extended practice has been for fund-raising of both cash and gifts-in-kind (GIK). The U.S. office maintains relationships with more than ninety corporations, and the tendency is to increase the number. Most GIK donations come from an excess of inventory and consist of products such as clothing, shoes, building materials, seeds, medical equipment and supplies, books, school supplies and food. Most of these donations are shipped to countries in Africa, Asia, Latin America and Eastern Europe. Some of the products also go to poor regions in the United States, such as Appalachia.[7]

Most corporations prefer that their cash donations go to specific domestic projects. One primary motivation for corporate giving is self-promotion and public relations. These companies are interested in their own constituencies. They also have specific geographic interests mainly where they are operating. Most of the money raised in the U.S. benefits people from the locale of those companies. Some corporations with transnational operations also contribute resources for relief and community development programs in developing countries.

New efforts and approaches

Some international NGOs have been active in advocacy work against child labor, damage to the environment, infant-formula production, exploitation of unprotected work forces in developing countries and other issues affecting corporate practice, particularly with companies working at a transnational level. The aim is to influence corporate and business practices to make them more socially aware and responsible and to help them better understand community perspectives on social and sustainable development.

Other experiences involve improving work force education; supporting orientation for parents regarding technology education in schools; and exchanging information with corporations in return for advertising the need to help children.

World Vision's Taiwan office currently partners with chain stores, travel agencies, insurance firms and banks. Some of these businesses promote our programs and campaigns and offer discounts to our sponsors, and some provide financial support for our campaigns. In exchange we provide them with receipts for tax deductions and publicity in our programs. Some corporations are interested in supporting specific programs in developing countries that deal with a particular problem, particularly needs for children and protection of the environment.

Staff in Costa Rica view the relationship with private companies as an opportunity to promote awareness among business executives about public policy issues so that these executives will in turn influence key political leaders regarding government policies that affect the poor.

The Chile office has initiated relationships with some private enterprises, yielding support for health and education programs, especially for children. Another experience involves working with women from the Training Center for Women Development (Chile) and local hotels, restaurants and food-processing plants, where women have the opportunity to put their training into practice.

Micro-enterprise development programs are a natural environment for promoting relations with business people and organizations. There have been some initiatives to promote investment in specific economic programs, especially from Christian businessmen.

Conflicting and overlapping interests

As shown in Figure 8–1, there is room for negotiation, collaboration and mutual support between NGOs and business organizations. Some of the interests conflict, others overlap. The challenge is to find common ground while maintaining our essential identity and a critical, albeit respectful stand.

NGO interests	Business interests
• Access funds (get higher return on investment)	• Tax deductions
• Good reputation and good name to fulfill mission of promoting development	• Good reputation and good name to continue making profits
• Influence business practices and codes of conduct	• Improve image and be more competitive
• Support business organizations to allocate funds more effectively (in helping the poor)	• Some want to help the poor, do something good
• Help business organizations understand long-term implications	• Profit-making on a long-term basis
• Raise business organizations' awareness about social, economic, spiritual and environmental problems, inviting them to be part of the solution	• Counter criticism from advocacy groups about methods and practices
• Raise public awareness about NGOs in association with certain companies	• Improve image and become more competitive through an association with NGOs and the causes they support, for example, children, the environment
• Influence political leaders and public policy through business leaders	• Have a better educated work force

Figure 8–1: Comparison of business and NGO interests.

Difficulties and obstacles in dealing with business organizations

Mission: The nature and mission of NGOs may not be enough to compel many business organizations to become involved. Two different sets of values are at stake. Business organizations may respond out of humanitarian or selfish motives. There are CEOs, however, who are open to a more integrated presentation.

Distrust: Business organizations could be suspicious of NGOs, especially because of NGO advocacy efforts, and may question the professional standards of NGOs.

Lack of knowledge about business organizations: NGOs lack knowledge and understanding about business organizations, especially about the large ones that operate at national and international levels.

Lack of structure, funding and expertise: Most NGOs lack the organizational structure to facilitate work with the business sector. At the same time there is a lack of staff with appropriate expertise to deal with business organizations beyond the fund-raising mode. Finally, most NGOs do not have funding to invest in this new initiative.

Lower rates of return: For NGOs, the rate of return on investment is very low compared to that of traditional fund-raising. Relationships with business organizations may not necessarily mean quick money. Investing in long-term relationships should be developed.

Quality of proposals: In some contexts business organizations have shown an interest in supporting specific projects, but their demands are high regarding the quality of the proposals. Traditional project designs do not meet their corporate standards.

Suggested next steps

Following are some concrete actions for moving forward in establishing relationships with the business sector:

Understand the business sector: An analysis of the business sector's nature, needs and interests is fundamental. This analysis should be precise about each economic sector represented by business organizations that are to be contacted. NGOs must choose which business organizations they want to establish relations with and for what specific reasons, and find out what approaches are appealing in each case. The analysis should be more comprehensive when dealing with transnational corporations.

Contextualize: No fixed rules apply in relationships with business organizations. Develop a strategy for each particular context. Even in relationships with transnational corporations, strategies should be contextualized to the realities of both the host society (communities) and the foreign company.

Develop a relationship of mutual respect: NGOs must cultivate long-term relationships at all levels with business organizations, even with organizations that are reluctant to engage in any form of association. NGOs need to gain respect so they can influence business practices and key business leaders. Of special and strategic interest is the ability to influence CEOs of large corporations in key sectors.

Develop internal capacity: NGOs need staff who know and understand the business sector and have the skills and abilities to relate with business people. Leaders of NGOs should understand the importance and potential of establishing relationships with business organizations and create the organizational conditions (structure, staff and funding) to support these efforts.

Build strategic alliances: Build strategic alliances on two levels. First, work with people in business organizations who can be advocates for partnering with NGOs. Second, partner with companies that are widely known for being socially and environmentally responsible and with value-based businesses as an entry to the larger sector.

Key role of board members: There is much that NGOs can learn from the business men and women who are members of their boards about how to develop strategies for partnering with business organizations. Board members can also play important roles in promoting relations beyond fund-raising.

Act as a global community: Sharing resources and experiences within the NGO community is an imperative. At the same time, NGOs in the North and South must learn to work together, especially when dealing with transnational corporations.

Serious and detailed planning: Relationships with business organizations demand a high degree of professionalism. In some cases these relationships may mean scaling-up at international levels involving different actors.

OTHER INITIATIVES

Other NGOs' experiences

Some NGOs have established partnerships with corporations and banks to open up credit programs, at a wider level, for micro-entrepreneurs, a sector previously neglected by governments, the banking system and multilateral organizations. Some of these NGOs are active in linking local banks with international banks. Others promote investment opportunities and connect international investors with small local business and grassroots groups. At the same time, these NGOs build strategic alliances with financial institutions to support micro-enterprise programs.

Another type of relationship concerns the practice of exchanging information and expertise. One NGO[8] working in promoting sustainable agriculture with peasants and farmers in developing countries has developed relationships with transnational corporations working on research in forestry and agriculture. The NGO benefits from corporate technical expertise on environmental protection programs, managing credit and loan programs, and business management in general. In exchange, the NGO helps CEOs of commercial banks and corporations understand the context of developing countries and sometimes asks executives to get involved personally in some development programs. CEOs travel at their own expense and spend time in villages, working with a cooperative or credit program, and sharing their business expertise with local leaders. This personal involvement is not common practice, but it is powerful for the following reasons: (1) it connects leaders of large corporations and commercial banks with grassroots leaders in developing countries; (2) it enriches the lives of the people involved; and (3) it creates multiple levels of collaboration among business leaders, community leaders and NGOs.

One NGO began a dialogue with large transnational corporations concerning social and environmental standards for producing agricultural products in developing countries. This NGO (1) assists local producers in developing countries with using production methods that are socially and environmentally sound; (2) imports and markets the products in its home country; (3) creates brands for products that are produced in socially and environmentally sound conditions; (4) participates in lobbying activities with governments and international organizations to enforce standards and codes of conduct for production and trade activities; and (5) negotiates with corporations through market pressure, with the aim of creating fair-trade conditions for producers in the South. This NGO works with a chain of more than 600 supermarkets in Europe. It believes in a business-to-business relationship with business organizations by intervening directly in the market. It works closely with consumers in its own society to raise awareness about production and trade conditions, and about regulations.

Initiatives by international and multilateral organizations

Both the United Nations, particularly UNICEF, and the World Bank promote "constructive cooperation" and "business partnerships for development" respectively (see UNICEF 1997; World Bank 1998). The State of the World's Children, UNICEF's annual report, provides concrete examples of "how critical a role the private sector can play, especially in an era of declining foreign aid" (UNICEF 1997, 64). Examples include involving NGOs in various types of partnerships with business organizations. UNICEF's experience "has shown that corporations can be receptive to change" and that there is hope for corporations to "shift from being a source of the problem to becoming part of the solution" (ibid., 65).

The World Bank's rationale for promoting business partnerships for development lies in the fact that

> the roles and responsibilities of business, civil society and state in development are changing and becoming more interdependent. We are moving from a world in which business maximized profits independently of the interests of society at large and the state was seen as sole provider and/or financier of the public good, to a world where success depends not just on complementarity of actions among business, civil society and state, but on synergy (World Bank 1998, 2).

Encouraging partnerships and relationships between NGOs and business organizations is being promoted by international and multilateral organizations, by governments, by NGOs and by other civil society groups. Each of these actors has a particular interest for engaging in collaboration and partnership with the other. The motives may be different, but there is room to work together and find common ground. As the document from the World Bank underscores, "Together, forward thinking leaders from the private sector, civil society and government are creating partnership activities which benefit the long-term interests of business while also the social objectives of civil society and of the state" (ibid.).

THE CHALLENGES AHEAD

The main challenge to building relationships between NGOs and business organizations will be to go beyond the fund-raising and traditional advocacy modes. The road ahead will not be free of obstacles and risks, and NGOs will have to analyze these carefully and develop strategies for each context. Following are some initial thoughts to consider; significant discussion needs to take place at different levels to make continued progress.

A conceptual point of departure: The inconstant and uneven nature of the current development system creates inequality, poverty and different types of vulnerabilities. NGOs face a complex situation in their efforts to promote alternative types of development, and the task ahead is greater than their current resources can sustain.

The business sector plays a key role in society and must become part of the solution to the problems we all face. Business organizations can participate in more meaningful ways than contributing money and gifts-in-kind. They have power, influence, financial resources, experience, the means to do research and technical expertise. Their business practices have both positive and negative impacts on society, and there is much that NGOs can do to enhance the positive impacts.

NGOs are in a privileged position to develop different types of relationships with business organizations, involving collaboration, negotiation, exchange of knowledge, pressure, partnership and alliance-building. In the process of building these relationships, however, NGOs should not compromise their essential mission and values to gain access to the financial resources available through business organizations. A transparent and respectful relation between NGOs and business organizations should result in finding common ground around issues that transcend both actors. The aim should be to benefit larger segments of society, mainly the poor and oppressed, as well as the environment.

Shaping the values and vision of the business sector: The main contribution NGOs can make to business organizations is to influence their set of values and shape their vision. The challenge will be to move beyond providing knowledge to assisting business organizations and CEOs in making judgments. What Fowler states is applicable in this situation:

What people need more than information is enough time, help and incentive to decide which values to sacrifice when values conflict with one another, as they do in development assistance. NGOs through their development education efforts have concentrated on informing people about the inhumane situation facing millions in the South and now the East. NGOs could play a significant role in educating citizens and corporations about the complex and slow process of self-improvement of development (1997, 216).

A relationship with business organizations should seek to influence behavior, practice, values and vision, incorporating elements of justice, sustainability and fair practice in production and trade. This does not mean that fund-raising should not play a part in relationships with business organizations, but NGOs should discover strategies to do fund-raising in a way that will not contradict their advocacy work.

The poor and the business sector: Another key actor and a historical partner of NGOs in the development process is the poor, including local communities and grassroots groups. The role of NGOs vis-à-vis the poor and business organizations would be to facilitate relationships, understanding and negotiation. Relationships with the business sector should not prevent NGOs from continuing to facilitate full participation of the poor in the development process. Strategies to bring the poor into relationship and dialogue with representatives from business organizations should be a goal of continued engagement with the business sector. NGOs would have to prepare community leadership to engage with the business sector by (1) facilitating access to information about the businesses involved; (2) providing technical support to community leaders so they can organize information about their own situation; (3) helping community leaders develop skills in public relations, marketing and negotiation; and (4) assisting community leaders by building confidence to engage in more horizontal—instead of paternalistic—relationships with business representatives.

Act as global organizations: Traditional NGO modes of operation will not contribute to a successful relationship with business organizations, especially when dealing with transnational corporations. The old paradigm of Northern NGOs playing fund-raising and advocacy roles, and Southern NGOs playing the role of recipients of funds and project managers, no longer conveys the true nature of the NGO world. In the North, NGOs are increasingly working with their domestic poor, and in the South NGOs engage in domestic fund-raising activities. There is poverty and concentration of wealth in both the North and the South.

Relationships with the business sector should take place in both the North and the South. NGOs should aim to engage in relationships with the business sector at the local, national and international level. This approach must bring together a variety of NGO staff working in fund-raising and marketing strategies with those working on advocacy activities and those working at the grassroots level. When dealing with transnational corporations a well-synchronized strategy should be developed involving key participants from the North and South.

The role of leadership: In large and complex NGOs, the role of leadership is key to promoting more effective ways of alternative and transformational development. It is leadership's responsibility to create the structure and resources necessary to engage in innovative practice, to expand vision on a long-term basis, and to provide support to explore possible frontiers.

CONCLUSIONS

The relationship between NGOs and business organizations involves more than just another strategy for fund-raising. It presents an opportunity to engage in innovative and more effective practices to cope with the problems of poverty, inequality and environmental damage in the North, the South, the East, and the West. Extensive discussions are needed to clarify the purpose of the relationship and the appropriate strategies relevant to each particular context. There is also a need to exchange and document experiences occurring in many places. Policies are needed to clarify NGO positions on relationships with business organizations and to provide guidelines for different entities around the world.

Notes

[1] "Business organizations" refers to for-profit organizations from the private sector, whose main interest is to maximize profit and accumulate wealth. They have different names in different parts of the world. I use "corporations" and "private enterprises" interchangeably.

[2] "In Australia there isn't a long tradition of philanthropy or corporate social responsibility as in the United States, but the sentiment for business social responsibility is increasing." Interview with Greg Thompson, World Vision Australia, April 16, 1998.

[3] See some references to corporate involvement in charity and philanthropy in Van der Ploeg and Sap 1995.

[4] "Social awareness is rising in private enterprises in Costa Rica; globalization is making them more competitive and is increasing their need to have better connections with poor communities." Interview with Arnoldo Valverde, World Vision Costa Rica, April 21, 1998.

[5] At the Threshold of the Third Millennium was a conference organized by both national and transnational private enterprises in Peru. One topic under discussion was the social responsibility of private enterprises (El Comercio, Lima, March 26, 1998).

[6] "Seventy percent of Dutch corporations have donated toward charity in the last 12 months (approx. US$100 million). Only 10% is given toward a Third World cause" (interview, Delhaas 1998). "Ideas of corporate responsibility are starting to permeate Australian society, especially concerning work with indigenous communities in

remote places in Australia" (interview, Greg Thompson, 1998). "Most of the money we raise is to benefit people from the locale of companies" (interview, Sam Jackson, 1998).

[7] A comprehensive research effort is needed to learn about the history and current practices of different types of relationships that NGOs have established and are presently establishing with business organizations worldwide. This chapter is limited to interviews with key staff in a few countries.

[8] This section contains the experiences of three NGOs, two based in Europe and one in the United States, working in Latin America.

Bibliography

Brandt, Don. 1997. "Are NGOs on the Road to Hell?" *Together* 56 (October–December).

Comelieu, Christian. 1996. "Au-dela de la Gestion." In *Impasses et Promesses: L'Ambiguite de la Cooperation au Development*, Nouveaux Cahiers de L'IUED 4. Geneva.

Commins, Stephen. 1997. "World Vision and Corporations in a Global Economy: Markets, Mental Models and Ministry," World Vision discussion paper (September).

De Brie. 1996. "L'Europe dans la nasse de l'austerité." *Le Monde Diplomatique* (July).

De Oliveira, Darcy, and Rajesh Tandon. 1994. *Citizens Strengthening Global Civil Society*. World Assembly Edition. Washington: CIVICUS World Alliance for Citizen Participation.

Edwards, Michael, and David Hulme. 1994. *Making a Difference: NGOs and Development in a Changing World*. Save the Children. London: Earthscan Publications Ltd.

Estes, Ralph. 1996. "Corporate Accountability: The Tyranny of the Bottom Line." *The World Business Academy Journal* 10, no. 1. San Francisco: Berret-Koehler Publishers.

Fowler, Alan. 1997. *Striking a Balance: A Guide to Enhancing the Effectiveness of Non-Governmental Organizations in International Development*. London: Earthscan Publications Ltd.

Friedmann, John. 1993. *Empowerment: The Politics of Alternative Development*. Cambridge USA and Oxford UK: Blackwell.

Friedmann, John, and Clyde Weaver. 1980. *Territory and Function: The Evolution of Regional Planning*. Berkeley and Los Angeles: University of California Press.

Kelleher, David, and Kate McLaren. 1996. *Grabbing the Tiger by the Tail: NGOs Learning for Organizational Change*. Canada: Canadian Council for International Co-operation.

Kolodner, Eric. 1994. *Transnational Corporations: Impediments or Catalysts of Social Development?* UNRISD Occasional Paper no. 5. Geneva: World Summit for Social Development.

Korten, David. 1990. *Getting to the 21ˢᵗ Century: Voluntary Action and the Global Agenda*. West Hartford, Conn.: Kumarian Press.

———. 1995. *When Corporations Rule the World*. West Hartford, Conn.: Kumarian Press; San Francisco: Berrett-Koehler Publishers.

Petras and Cavaluzi. 1996. "On peut devenir pauvre en travaillant." *Le Courrier* (July).

Storper, Michael, and Richard Walker. 1989. *The Capitalist Imperative: Territory, Technology, and Industrial Growth*. Cambridge USA and Oxford UK: Blackwell.

UNICEF. 1997. "The Private Sector: Part of the Solution." *The State of the World's Children 1997*. Oxford University Press.

Van der Ploeg, Tymen, and John W. Sap, eds. 1995. *Rethinking the Balance: Government and Non-Governmental Organizations in the Netherlands*. Amsterdam: VU University Press.

Villacorta, Corina. 1997a. "Emergent Roles of NGOs: The Relationship with the Business For-Profit Sector." Master's thesis. Los Angeles: University of California.

————. 1997b. "Non-Governmental Organizations Are Changing: A Perspective from Latin America." *UNRISD NEWS* [The United Nations Research Institute for Social Development Bulletin] 16 (Spring/Summer). Geneva.

World Bank. 1998. "Development Grant Facility Funding New Grant Proposal for FY 1998." (January).

PART FIVE

CONCLUSION

9

What Have We Learned?

Beris Gwynne

In a world that seems to have gone amok—where evil and injustice breed and feed new generations of evil and injustice, obscuring signs of "progress"—what is certain is that good works alone will not eradicate poverty or injustice if hearts, systems, political and economic structures are not reconciled and restored.

If the subversion of God's original intention in creation can be identified as the cause of all poverty and injustice, then God's redemptive plan not only explains the origins of poverty but provides the solutions—ultimately offering *the* unifying theme for our earthly existence: we are stewards of God's creation. Conceivably, no human endeavor could be considered outside this framework. Because all of creation represents an interdependent system, efforts to address poverty and injustice must begin with a holistic framework, not a piecemeal substitute. What this requires of us—the integration of faith and life, faith and work in every aspect of our being—can readily be applied to the Christian church as a whole. Doing so puts our presence and ministry on earth into perspective, reminds us of our part in God's plan and calls us all to holistic living at home and abroad.

TRUE INTEGRATION DOESN'T COME EASILY

Christian humanitarian aid workers are quick to acknowledge their faith as the primary motivation for their work. We describe our relief and development work as a response to God's salvation/restoration plan ("For God so loved the world . . . " [John 3:16]). The Bible and Jesus' example are our "operating instructions" for service and witness—for advice on what to do, how to do it, and applicable to all we do—whether emergency relief and disaster mitigation, child- or family- or community-focused development, advocacy, micro-enterprise economic development or fund-raising. (Even our pleas for humanitarian giving in marketing and communications material should speak to supporters about relief and development and advocacy work in the context of God's redemptive/restoration plan.)

But true integration of faith and daily life doesn't come easily, especially to development workers whose training and formation reflect Western culture and mindsets that separate the physical and spiritual worlds and laud rational, technology-based remedies. We find it easy to respond to the command to minister to others in Christ's name—to heal the sick, feed the hungry, free the captive, and so on. But many of us struggle to find God in the midst of grinding poverty, often horrific injustice and wanton cruelty. Instead of the reign of love, we find ourselves living under the all-too-human reign of competition for resources, in which power is misused to exploit and marginalize.

Our attempt in this book has been to challenge the church's understanding of poverty and its origins, and to place our poor efforts to bring significant and lasting change (transformational development) in the context of God's redemptive plan. Not merely "about" or "of" or "for" the poor, but God's own work, to which he calls his followers on the world's behalf, across nationality, race, socioeconomic status, culture and gender, to take up the Genesis call as guardians and stewards of all creation.

RESTORING A BROKEN WORLD

This call translates into more than just good works or charity—food for the hungry, water for the thirsty, and so on (traditional relief and development activities). It incorporates the call to attitudes and behaviors that respect and actively seek to promote human rights based on God-given worth and dignity, to advocate for justice, as well as generous and merciful consideration of others and less concern for self. Such an approach embraces spiritual, physical and social/emotional dimensions. It integrates disaster mitigation and emergency relief activities in sustainable community development for long-term impact and effectiveness.

This redemptive call institutes the reign of acceptance, forgiveness, love and justice. Transformational development, then, is fundamentally about restoring right relationships and fellowship in the context of God's creation and worldview. Our part is to live under the reign of God's kingdom. This is development work that truly transforms, that truly restores hope.

APPLICATION TO ALL CHRISTIANS

Learnings from these chapters apply not only to relief and development work in the "developing world," but also to transformational development in the "developed world." When Jayakumar Christian questions common assumptions about the nature of poverty, he leads us to see that the identity of rich and poor alike is marred by sin and separation from God. Rich and poor play a part in perpetuating unjust practices and behaviors, locking whole peoples into intergenerational poverty. In accepting "the way things are," the rich bear witness to their own marred identity in relation to God's plan and fail to fulfill their responsibilities to "the least" (Matt. 24). Dr. Christian challenges relief and development professionals to consider the possibility that we ourselves might be guilty of "seeking to play God in the lives of the poor"—unwitting co-conspirators with political and economic structures and other powerful forces who are the purveyors of history, information and opinion, perpetuating injustice and poverty.

Other chapters bear witness to the gospel's demand for organizational and management models that transcend 19th-century paradigms (North/South, donor/recipient, dollar-driven support/dollar-deprived field). Servant leadership, defined by the life of Jesus, implies a challenge to all lifestyles. This book's treatment of Appreciative Inquiry in "healing the marred image of the poor" speaks as much to aid agencies' public relations and marketing managers as to relief and development practitioners. I believe it speaks equally well to churches about discipleship.

Siobhan O'Reilly's work provides compelling evidence to support the proposition that, in the very process of providing for the needs of children and their families, holistic Christian community development provides a firm foundation for conflict prevention, conflict intervention and resolution and peace-making. More intentional integration of peace-building in thousands of community-development projects could reasonably be expected to bear significant fruit.

Need for better understanding of the structural and systemic characteristics of the global economy is outlined in chapters on micro-enterprise development and on corporate sector engagement. In an era when large transnational corporations rival, even outstrip, many nations in size of economies and global networks, complex challenges continue to frustrate collective best intentions to reduce poverty and seek more equitable distribution of the world's resources. Many of the ideas and recommendations in this book beg to be explored further.

WHERE DO WE GO FROM HERE?

Clearly, no one among us is exempt from the command "to do justice, to love mercy, and to walk humbly" with God (Mic. 6:8). Clearly, too, learnings and suggestions of what this may mean for the mission of the church at large, from development and relief professionals in a Christian context, need to reach a broader audience. Opportunities must be taken to bear witness to personal encounters with God and God's redemptive plan for the world, and the "manual of instructions" contained in Scripture and incarnate in Jesus Christ. We must ask more of ordinary Christians, that they would engage more significantly with the heart of the gospel. Do we do this through leadership training? Through church leadership and theologians? Where does the conversation go?

In addition, there is room for much more deliberate thinking about children. About their place in God's plan. About what Jesus says they can teach us. Perhaps this wisdom of the child's worldview can assist in our efforts to restore community and better design community-development processes. The status of children is the best measure of well-being, right relationships and joyful anticipation of the future.

We must also be more deliberate in making sure the voices of the poor are heard, directly whenever possible, and accurately in any case. The God we follow has always used stories to illustrate, inspire and provide windows to the truth. But we dare not, as development workers, "appropriate" stories of the poor in a way that disempowers or distorts God's view of things. Scripture Search, as described in this work, urges greater use of storytelling, drama and parables, drawing us always back to the original Story while also revealing interesting connections between worldview and resulting interpretations of that Story. Further work in understanding implications for mainstream and indigenous theology would be helpful. We must, at every step of the way, resist the temptation to triumphalism, which threatens true deepening of faith and understanding.

Finally, any careful reader will conclude that for each discussion that began with each chapter, there is a corresponding need for further research, better documentation of use of tools in the field, collection of emerging evidence and dissemination of lessons learned. Because our work and mission occur in the context of such overwhelming need, it is difficult to protect space for these investments, just as it is to protect time and space for prayer, reflection, meditation and other God-ordained necessities in the face of organizational pressures to measure performance by more "concrete" outcomes.

It's difficult to imagine any enterprise of life wherein exploring God's intentions and redemptive plan for the world could not speak to us. We have so far to go, but this same God promises to sustain us.

World Vision

Other Titles from World Vision Publications

Walking With the Poor: Principles and Practices of Transformational Development by Bryant L. Myers.

The author says those who want to alleviate poverty need to walk with the poor, see their reality, and then look for solutions. He explores Christian views of poverty and looks at how it is experienced in different cultures. Draws on theological and biblical resources as well as secular development theory and practice to develop a theoretical framework for working alongside the poor. 288 pp. **$21.95**

Serving With the Urban Poor: Cases in Holistic Ministry, Tetsunao Yamamori, Bryant L. Myers & Kenneth Luscombe, eds.

Case studies from around the world focus on the plight of the urban poor and show how they can come to know the hope of Christ and progress beyond their physical needs. 248 pp. **$16.95**

Serving With the Poor in Africa: Cases in Holistic Ministry, Tetsunao Yamamori, Bryant L. Myers, Kwame Bediako & Larry Reed, eds.

Holism in Africa means something different than it does in Latin America or elsewhere. The case studies presented here reveal the nature and complexities of effective Christian holistic ministry in various African contexts. 240 pp. **$15.95**

Serving With the Poor in Asia: Cases in Holistic Ministry, Tetsunao Yamamori, Bryant L. Myers & David Conner, eds.

Analyzing several cases of holistic ministry from throughout Asia, leading mission thinkers Paul Hiebert, Edgar Elliston, Vinay Samuel and others show how holism powerfully impacts anthropology, leadership training, theology, management and strategic mission planning. 216 pp. **$15.95**

Toll Free in the U.S.: 1-800-777-7752

Direct: (626) 301-7720

Web: www.marcpublications.com

World Vision Publications • 800 W. Chestnut Ave. • Monrovia, CA • 91016

Ask for a complete publications catalog and free missions newsletter